# THE LIGHT IS STILL SHINING

# THE LIGHT IS STILL SHINING

## The Gospel Of John For A Troubled World

*by*

STUART R. OGLESBY, D.D.

Author of *"Prayers for All Occasions," "Becoming a Member of the Presbyterian Church," "The Baby Is Baptized,"* etc.

NEW YORK
FLEMING H. REVELL COMPANY
LONDON AND EDINBURGH

Copyrighted, MCMXLIV, by
Fleming H. Revell Company

This book has been manufactured in this form in compliance with orders of the War Production Board for the conservation of paper and other materials necessary for the prosecution of the War.

Printed in the United States of America

Quotations from the American Standard Edition of the Revised Bible are used by permission of the International Council of Religious Education.

New York: 158 Fifth Avenue
London: 16 Anerley Hill

# CONTENTS

|  |  |  |
|---|---|---|
| I. | THE LIGHT IS STILL SHINING | 7 |
| II. | JESUS WAS THERE | 13 |
| III. | THE DEEP THINGS OF GOD | 18 |
| IV. | HE MUST NEEDS GO THROUGH SAMARIA | 27 |
| V. | WILT THOU BE MADE WHOLE? | 37 |
| VI. | DOWN FROM HEAVEN | 43 |
| VII. | WILLING PLUS DOING EQUALS KNOWING | 51 |
| VIII. | LIGHT AND TRUTH | 61 |
| IX. | ONE THING I KNOW | 68 |
| X. | THE DOOR | 77 |
| XI. | RESURRECTION AND LIFE | 86 |
| XII. | SONS OF LIGHT | 99 |
| XIII. | AND IT WAS NIGHT | 106 |
| XIV. | ARISE, LET US GO HENCE | 114 |
| XV. | YE ARE MY FRIENDS, IF — | 121 |
| XVI. | OVERCOMING THE WORLD | 130 |
| XVII. | JESUS' PRAYER FOR PEACE | 137 |
| XVIII. | DARKNESS AT ITS WORST | 147 |
| XIX. | CRUCIFIED, DEAD AND BURIED | 156 |
| XX. | GOOD MORNING! | 166 |
| XXI. | AN IMPERISHABLE POSTSCRIPT | 175 |

# I
## THE LIGHT IS STILL SHINING

Two well-known Englishmen, one a Foreign Secretary and one a King, have spoken words about light which have found permanent lodgment in the mind and heart of the English-speaking world. Twenty-five years intervened between these two utterances which, given from different viewpoints, have both been proven by experience to be profoundly true.

In his autobiography, "After Twenty-Five Years," Viscount Edward Grey describes the night of August 3, 1914. It was the day that Great Britain had declared war on Imperial Germany. He and some of his friends were looking out of the window of the Foreign Office, No. 10 Downing Street, just at dawn. They saw the lights being turned out in that part of London and Grey turned to his companions, saying, "The lamps are going out now all over Europe. We shall not see them lit again in our lifetime."

The First World War was fought and won after four hard years by Britain and her allies. The years following witnessed the failure to establish a lasting and just peace. The Armistice of November 11, 1918, never became anything more than an armistice — a temporary cessation of armed conflict. In September, 1939, fighting on a world scale began and Britain stood with her back to the wall, as she had never been forced to stand during the previous war. It was then, in his New Year's message to the British Empire, that King George VI, quoting from a little-known poet, said: "I said to a man who stood at the gate of the year: 'Give me a light that I may tread safely into the unknown.' And he replied, 'Go out into the darkness and put your hand into the hand of God. That shall be to you better than a light and safer than a known way.'" These words of Christian faith put new heart into the hard-pressed peoples of the United Nations.

The Apostle John also has something to say about darkness and light in the opening verses of his account of the gospel. In verses four and five of the first chapter, we read: "In him was life and the life was the light of men. And the light shineth in darkness; and the darkness comprehended it not." These words take on a new and striking meaning for us when they are changed from their seventeenth-century form to the language we speak today. Dr. Edgar J. Goodspeed does this in his translation of the New Testament when he renders them: "The light is still shining in the darkness, for the darkness has never put it out." Some years ago, after hearing Dr. Goodspeed lecture, I attended an informal reception in his honor. At that time, I thanked him warmly for this translation which had meant so much to me. He replied simply: "I translated the verse that way, because that is what I believe the Apostle meant!"

In the troubled world in which we live, we should all be deeply grateful and profoundly encouraged as we grasp the truth that darkness has never put out that

Light and can never do so, now or in the ages to come. Lights may go out, but it is not darkness which causes them to stop shining. And the Light which lighteth every man, whose coming into the world John describes so effectively, can never be put out, nor will it go out of Itself, for it is the Light of God.

The first witness of the Light whom the Apostle introduces is John, elsewhere called, because of his type of ministry, John the Baptist. John, being the last of the Old Testament prophets and the first of the New Testament preachers, stood one day on the banks of the River Jordan and, pointing to Jesus, preached the first gospel sermon: "Behold the Lamb of God, which taketh away the sin of the world." No recorded results of that sermon are given, but on the next day the same sermon was preached and the same words were used. This time two of John's disciples turned and followed Jesus. Thus, as he had foretold, John began to decrease as Jesus began to increase.

There are here two very plain and practical truths taught and illustrated which Christian workers have been slow to grasp. The first is that one should never be content with a single effort at witnessing for Jesus and never be discouraged when that effort apparently is without results. The cumulative effect of two testimonies expressed in identical words in winning two disciples for the Master is purposely given and must not be forgotten when we do personal work.

The other is the harder of the two truths to accept. It is that the disciple must always decrease when His Master increases. John the Baptist made no objection to his two friends leaving him to follow Jesus. He must have encouraged them to do so. There was no ambition in the heart of John except that directed toward the Kingdom and the King. Too often Christian workers show the opposite of this spirit of true humility, and while those who do so may win many followers, and receive much attention and praise, let them know that only he who exalts his Master and seeks no glory for himself is really advancing the cause of Christ and hastening the coming of His final triumph.

John and Andrew, for those were the names of the new disciples of Jesus, immediately went to work for Him. John sought his brother James, and Andrew brought his brother Peter to Jesus. The day following, Jesus Himself finds Philip and calls him into the newly-formed little company. Philip then sets out to do his first bit of personal work and gave his testimony to his friend Nathanael: "We have found him of whom Moses in the law, and the prophets did write, Jesus of Nazareth, the son of Joseph." Nathanael was not easily convinced but, accepting the challenge to come and see, he became the sixth member of the Apostolic group.

This first chapter of John has been called the great personal-work chapter of the New Testament. Two men were won to Jesus through the preaching of John the Baptist, one became a disciple because Jesus spoke to him directly, and three were brought to Jesus through the personal testimony of their friends. It would be straining the meaning of the narrative to say that this proportion was intended to be maintained through subsequent centuries. But it is nothing less than failure to recognize the truth when we see it if we do not acknowledge the importance of one man's witnessing to his friend the eternal truths he himself has learned.

And now the Light is shining in and from six men whose number is soon to be increased to twelve, and later to be still further enlarged by the addition of others, both men and women. But what are twelve men, or one hundred and twenty men and women, in a world where millions live who have not seen the Light and who love darkness rather than light because their deeds are evil? Just here, at the very beginning of the Christian Era, we may find strong encouragement as we face the darkness that is still widespread in the world twenty centuries later. The powers of darkness did not put out the Light in this little band. Danger, persecution, imprisonment, even death itself, only caused the Light to shine more brightly. Down through the centuries it has been shining. More and more widely scattered throughout the earth are found those whose lives have been lighted and whose greatest yearning desire is to lead others to the Light.

No enterprise in all the history of the world has enlisted more men and women in its service than that which was begun on the banks of the Jordan when John pointed to Jesus and said, "Behold the Lamb of God." No cause has called forth more devotion or more sacrificial effort than that of spreading the good tidings of great joy which is available for all people.

In 1937, a great Ecumenical Conference was held in Oxford, England. Representatives from every nation on earth were present. If there was a single nation or land upon the face of the globe which did not have some one in that great Christian gathering to represent it and to speak for it, the fact was not revealed to the less influential delegates present, of whom the writer was one. It was a conference on "Life and Work." Much time, thought and prayer were spent on the important matter of Church unity and how it might be promoted. But the fact that impressed and amazed this delegate was the amount and quality of Christian unity already in existence throughout the world. While the conference was in progress the "Shanghai Incident" occurred and Japan began the invasion of China. Yet Chinese and Japanese delegates sat on the platform as citizens of an eternal kingdom and men in whom the Light was shining, without any disruption of their Christian fellowship. The Second World War was then beginning, if, indeed, it had not already started years before when Japan invaded Manchuria or when certain great nations sent their arms and fighting men into Spain. But in spite of this darkness and all the increased darkness that was threatening, the Light shone more brightly than at any similar world conference held since the beginning of the Christian Era.

Let the powers of darkness do their worst. The heavens are now open and the angels of God are ascending and descending upon the Son of man and upon all who are His followers. If God be for us, who can be against us? The Light that lighteth every man will never go out!

## II

## JESUS WAS THERE

It is not without significance that John placed at the very beginning of his carefully selected list of eight miracles of Jesus to be recorded in his Gospel, the incident that occurred at the Marriage Feast in Cana of Galilee. This miracle was not first in point of time, for others had been performed previously. Nor was it first in importance. It must, therefore, have been first by design.

It is also significant to note, and to remember, that John always speaks of the miracles of Jesus as signs. Other gospel writers use different words interchangeably. John invariably uses the word that means "sign." He selects carefully eight miracles of Jesus out of all those with which he was familiar and writes them down as signs of the deity of Christ, signs that the Light which lighteth every man had come into the world. In the order that John relates them, they are: (1) changing water into wine, Chapter 2; (2) healing the nobleman's son at Capernaum, Chapter 4; (3) healing the impotent man at the pool of Bethesda, Chapter 5; (4) feeding the five thousand, Chapter 6; (5) walking on the sea, Chapter 6; (6) healing the man born blind, Chapter 9; (7) raising Lazarus from the dead, Chapter 11; (8) Christ's resurrection, Chapter 20. In the closing verse of the twentieth chapter, we read: "And many other signs truly did Jesus in the presence of his disciples, which are not written in this book: but these are written that ye might believe that Jesus is the Christ, the Son of God; and that believing ye might have life through his name."

The Marriage Feast in Cana is forever engraved on the hearts of Christians because Jesus was there and because of the miracle He performed. I have been to weddings where I felt sure Jesus was not present. I have been to other weddings where I was very sure He was present and that His Presence brought joy and happiness which the future trials and sorrows of life would not be able to destroy. Happy is that couple who do not forget to call Jesus to their marriage.

The fact that Jesus entered into the joyous and festive occasions held during His time should rebuke us if the quality of our Christianity is gloomy and cheerless. Too often we have a tendency to place ourselves in the same category with that austere Christian who remarked after he had eaten his first dish of ice cream that he knew it must be a sin to eat ice cream, for nothing in this life could be so good without sin being attached to it! Jesus was present at the marriage feast, and when the wine gave out because more guests arrived than were expected — perhaps it was Jesus and His six disciples who caused the unexpected demand on the prepared refreshments — He provided more wine by means of His divine power.

The difficulty of expressing in an entirely different and modern language what was said originally in a language two thousand years ago is strikingly illustrated in this incident. When the mother of Jesus reported to Him that there was no more wine, Jesus replied, according to the King James Version with which people are most familiar: "Woman, what have I to do with thee? Mine hour is not yet come." This sounds to us dangerously near to discourtesy if not disrespect. But it really was not so at all. Somewhere I read this paraphrase of His words, which seems to me to express just what He must have said: "That's all right, mother. I'll take care of the situation when the time comes." His mother showed no more anxiety after He had spoken to her, and she at once instructed the servants to do whatever He told them to do.

The praise the governor of the feast bestowed upon the wine into which water had been changed by the Master's power is convincing. There was no trickery about what was done. There was no substitution of something which was called wine. The miracle was genuine and the testimony adequate. In speaking of the miracle, Browning uses these beautiful words: "Conscious water saw her Lord and blushed!"

And still, today, men and women may call Jesus, not only to their marriages, but to all the social life in which they take part. What a purifying effect He would have in our lives if we were as conscious of His presence during our joys and pleasures through the week as we are of His presence in the church on Sunday, when we go to worship in company with our Christian brethren!

In this second chapter of John, we also see Jesus

in His contact with the world of business where dishonesty, cheating and special privilege were flourishing unrebuked and unashamed. The account is called the Cleansing of the Temple. It was that, but it was more than a forceful rebuke to those who would use the House of God for a place of profit. Jesus also, in this scene, rebuked once and forever those who exploit the people and take advantage of their need to make more profit than is just.

It was necessary in those days that pilgrims who came from outside Judea to worship in the Temple obtain Jewish coins in exchange for the Roman coins they would ordinarily bring with them, in order to pay the Temple tax. It was also necessary that sacrificial animals be provided for the large numbers who would crowd Jerusalem at the time of the great feasts. So Annas, the head of the high priestly caste, had obtained the Temple concessions and placed within the Temple courts what were known as the "booths of Annas." At these booths, Roman money could be changed into Jewish coins, and animals for sacrifice could be purchased. Such transactions *inside* the Temple would have been bad enough if the business had been conducted in a fair and honest way. But Annas exacted all the profits the traffic would bear. The whole set-up was detested by the Jewish people, but they did not dare do anything about it on account of their fear of the power of the house of Annas.

Jesus had been in the Temple many times before and had seen this nefarious business being carried on. He had said and done nothing before this because

His hour had not come. Now He was entering the Temple as a "son of the law," as a man with the full authority of maturity. More than that, He was entering as the long expected Messiah. Therefore He could no longer overlook this abuse. He made a whip of small cords and, with righteous indigation flashing from His face, drove the whole miserable crowd out of the Temple, saying: "Take these things hence; make not my Father's house an house of merchandise."

We would do well to remember the actions and the reactions of Jesus in this scene. Here we do not find a "gentle Jesus, meek and mild." We find One whose displeasure is written in every feature of His countenance and whose patience had reached its limit. Righteous indignation and anger broke forth into action as He saw the profaning of His Father's house and the cheating of the people by those who should have been their leaders in all things good. Those who think of Jesus as kindly and forgiving must remember also that He not only cleansed the Temple, but pronounced terrible judgments upon the cities of the plains and awful woes upon the scribes and Pharisees who were hypocrites. There is no encouragement in the gospel of Jesus of Nazareth for dishonesty, hypocrisy or injustice, whether in the Church, or out of it.

At the conclusion of the chapter, we read that Jesus did not trust Himself to the people who believed on Him at that time because of the miracles they had seen. "Because," continues John, "he knew all men, and needed not that any should testify of man: for he knew what was in man."

It is both reassuring and disconcerting to realize that Jesus knows what is in me without my telling Him and without any report from my friends or my enemies. In the gospel records Jesus always dealt with men with "complete sureness of touch." Nothing was hidden from Him and nothing deceived Him. And so it is with men and women in every age. They may have deceived themselves; they may have deceived their friends; they have never deceived Jesus.

Therefore, the question of supreme importance that we should ask ourselves as we meditate on the truths of this chapter is: In my social life, and in my business life, does He trust Himself to me?

## III

## THE DEEP THINGS OF GOD

A YOUNG man of my congregation was inducted into the army and in course of time was assigned to the duty of assistant to the chaplain in the camp where he was stationed. After serving in this assignment for some weeks, he wrote me frankly that he had never thought that preachers had much to do in their job, but now he didn't see how they ever got around to their many duties.

All earnest religious workers are busy, sometimes entirely too busy for their own good and for the good of the people to whom they minister. It is a burden which they should learn to bear patiently, that each day they must deliberately choose what they shall try to do and what they shall not even attempt. Those who are in positions of prominent leadership cannot give all the time desired of them by people who come for conferences, for instruction and for advice. Even Jesus, when He was on earth, had limitations which He had voluntarily accepted when He became man. His days had the same number of hours as the days of ordinary men, and He had the limited physical strength of a man of flesh.

The country where Jesus lived was small and densely populated. After His ministry began and He had performed some of His miracles, His fame spread abroad and the people flocked to Him. Mark tells us that Jesus on one occasion said to His disciples: "Come ye yourselves apart unto a desert place, and rest a while." Then the evangelist adds: "For there were many coming and going, and they had no leisure so much as to eat."

Nicodemus is introduced in the third chapter of John as a ruler of the Jews. He was thus a prominent leader of the church of his day and a man of influence and authority. When Jesus asked him during their conference: "Art thou the teacher of Israel, and understandest not these things?" (R.V.), He indicated by the words He used that Nicodemus was the outstanding teacher of his day. This being so, it was not merely fear for his reputation that caused him to come to Jesus by night. He sought a time when he might sit down and talk out the matters on his mind and heart without the distraction of a crowd and the interruption of thoughtless questions from others. It may be that he did not care to mix with the motley mob that often surrounded the Master, but this was only a minor motive for coming by night. People who were attracted to Jesus by curiosity or by the miracles of wonder would be resting and sleeping elsewhere after the sun had set. Only one who was deeply concerned spiritually would deprive himself of needed rest to set his mind at peace about religious matters. In later chapters of the Gospel we find that Nicodemus was a man of deep conviction and did not hesitate to incur the wrath and ridicule of the Sanhedrin when a principle was at stake (see chapter 7:50), nor the disapproval of both the ecclesiastical and Roman authorities when it came to assisting in the burial of Jesus. (See chapter 19:39.)

The conversation between Jesus and this doctor of the law is simple, yet, at the same time, so profound that none has been able to exhaust the riches of the truths Jesus revealed. Nicodemus began by paying an ungrudging compliment to Jesus: "We know thou art a teacher come from God, for no man can do these miracles which thou doest except God be with him." The reply of Jesus was as startling as it was unexpected: "Verily, verily, I say unto thee, except a man be born again, he cannot see the kingdom of God." Nicodemus, thinking in terms of physical birth, was incredulous, but Jesus quickly explained that He was speaking, not of physical birth, but of spiritual. There are many things in everyday life one cannot explain. In the time of Nicodemus, wind was more of a mystery than it is today, and wind was used by Jesus as an illustration. In Hebrew, Greek and Latin the same word is used for "breath," "spirit" and "wind." The Hebrew Scriptures that Nicodemus knew so well taught that God breathed into man the breath of life and man became a living soul. So Jesus, according to His custom, was teaching truth here by means of a parable which was peculiarly adapted for His purpose in dealing with Nicodemus.

When the prominent teacher of Israel still professed not to understand what was being said, Jesus replied, almost in amazement: "Art thou the teacher of Israel and knowest not these things? Verily, verily, I say unto thee we speak that we do know, and testify that we have seen and ye receive not our witness. If I have told you of earthly things and ye believe not, how shall ye believe, if I tell you of heavenly things?"

The short account of this conversation evidently does not contain all that was said, nor all the things Jesus told this man. It is necessary to read between the lines and the verses to understand the difference Jesus here makes between earthly and heavenly things. Nicodemus had spoken of "these miracles," indicating that the mighty works of Jesus already had become both numerous and well known. Jesus must have pointed out some of these and explained how He had healed the broken-hearted, preached deliverance to the captives of sin, opened the eyes of the blind and set at liberty them that were bruised. It was the man's inability to understand and accept these things that made Jesus doubtful of his ability to understand

and accept the heavenly things He was yet to reveal.

Let us give our attention first to the earthly things about which Jesus was speaking, and then consider the heavenly things which cannot be seen with human eyes, and can be revealed only by Him who came down from heaven.

## Earthly Things

The "earthly things" Jesus speaks of must have been the miracles of grace and power that had taken place already in His ministry, some of which Nicodemus himself must have seen. There was both a short-range and a long-range aspect of the work of Jesus on earth. The first had to do with His compassionate spirit in the relief of immediate need. He went about doing good and healing. But He was not a leader with no long range plans and no grand strategy, as John seemed to believe He was when he sent the message to Him from prison: "Art thou he that should come, or look we for another?" The long-range strategy was too deep for the prophet to fathom, even though he was the greatest of those born of women. This belonged to the "heavenly things" that Jesus alone understood and could reveal.

Though it is not possible to say just what the earthly things were about which Jesus talked to Nicodemus, we cannot be far wrong if we identify them with the miracles He had performed. Let us take the list that Jesus Himself gave in His reply to John: "The blind see, the lame walk, the lepers are cleansed, the deaf hear, the dead are raised, to the poor the gospel is preached." All these things had been done by the Master within sight of men. Thus they were earthly things though they were done with heavenly power. Nicodemus had difficulty in accepting what he had seen with his own eyes because he could not understand nor explain it.

It is the glory of the gospel today that it still has the power to accomplish wonders on earth that cannot be explained in ordinary terms. And it is our own lack of faith that there are not more of these miracles of grace in our churches and among those to whom we minister in Christ's name. Go to any rescue mission, if you want your faith strengthened, and see men who have been lifted out of clutches of sin and saved by grace to lives of unselfishness and service. Make the acquaintance of an "Alcoholics Anonymous" group and let them point out to you upstanding men and women, formerly drunken sots who had been given up as hopeless by physicians, psychiatrists, friends and even ministers of the gospel. Go to a penal institution where real religious work is carried on and look with awe upon formerly hardened criminals whom the gospel of Christ has saved from the bondage of sin. Such experiences will convince you not only that men must be born again to enter the Kingdom of Heaven, but that men are being born again and are entering that Kingdom.

There are illustrations of this truth that come closer home to us than those just mentioned. Here is a man who is not in an institution and is considered a success in life, as the world counts success. But he is not a whole man, he is definitely unhappy and unadjusted. He is subject to moods of depression, and his lack of self-control causes unhappiness to many, chiefly among the members of his own family. He himself grows more and more depressed and often thinks seriously of suicide. Is there any hope for him? Can he enter the Kingdom of Heaven? "Verily, I say unto you, ye must be born again." There are many, whom every pastor knows, who have been born again from frustrated, unhappy lives to lives of service and satisfaction by the power of God through faith.

Similar illustrations might be multiplied, but these are sufficient to make us understand the earthly things about which Jesus spoke and to realize that only our unbelief makes them infrequent. According to your faith be it done unto you.

## Heavenly Things

The heavenly things in the conversation of Jesus with Nicodemus refer to the long-range purposes of Christ's redemptive work and take us back into the councils of eternity where the plan of salvation sprang from the love of God. Only He that came down from heaven could reveal the things that took place in heaven.

Beginning with the fourteenth verse of the chapter, Jesus tells Nicodemus about these heavenly things. "As Moses lifted up the serpent in the wilderness, even so must the Son of man be lifted up." God's remedy for sin was the lifting up of His Son, not that He might be honored, but that He might be slain and in

His death pay the penalty for the sin of the world.

Nicodemus was quite familiar with the historical reference Jesus used. The Israelites in the wilderness had murmured against God so that He sent fiery serpents among them as a punishment. Whosoever was bitten by one of these serpents died in agony. When the people cried out to Moses for help, the Lord directed him to make a serpent of brass, place it on a pole and lift it up in the camp where the people could see it. "And it came to pass, that if a serpent had bitten any man, when he beheld the serpent of brass, he lived." (See Numbers 21:4 ff.)

It was not a bitten Israelite whose image was lifted up but a serpent, not a victim but the evil itself. Thus Paul declares that God hath made Him (Jesus) to be sin for us, who knew no sin, that we might be made the righteousness of God in Him. The one perfect man who ever lived was lifted up as sin, and as sin slain, so that those who look unto Him and believe may be saved from eternal death. Mankind could never have known this deep and mysterious truth except it had been revealed by Jesus Himself.

The sixteenth verse, called the Golden Text of the Bible, unfolds to us the love of God that was so great as to cause Him to give His only begotten Son for the salvation of the world. The seventeenth verse declares that God did not send His Son into the world to condemn the world, but that the world through Him might be saved.

These verses are so familiar to Bible students they need little explanation. There are, however, two aspects of the truth here revealed that we need to keep more clearly before our minds. God loved the world, not just one man or one group of men in the world. And He sent His Son that the world might be saved. There are many places in the Bible where individual salvation is spoken of. Here it is the salvation of the world that Jesus declared He came to accomplish. What this includes it is not possible nor necessary to set down here. But we should realize that it includes infinitely more than our finite minds can understand. A saved man in a wicked world does not fulfill the promise. A saved man in a saved world approaches more nearly the meaning of Jesus' words. When we begin to think of what this means we can sing understandingly:

> "Transported with the view, I'm lost
> In wonder, love, and praise!"

The other truth which needs to be continually refreshed in our minds is that Jesus came not to condemn the world but to save the world. Now, condemnation is, at times, necessary and proper. But the Church has been too often on the condemnation side with reference to the world. The world must have been worth saving, or Christ would not have come to save it. The world must be capable of being saved, or Christ's mission was futile, judged according to His own words to Nicodemus. Those who love darkness rather than light are already under condemnation. But the Light is still shining in the darkness, and our faith, when we catch the long-range promise of this passage, is that the time will come when more men on earth love light than love darkness. This faith will hold us steady when darkness seems to be in the ascendency over the earth. The heavenly things that Jesus has revealed to us give us spiritual courage and enable us to say from the depths of hearts made strong and pure by a new birth: "Bless the Lord, O my soul, and all that is within me, bless his holy name!"

## IV

## HE MUST NEEDS GO THROUGH SAMARIA

THE MINISTRY of Jesus in Judea was brief and unsuccessful. Turning away from the hostility of the people who ought to have been eager and anxious to receive Him — it was His own who received Him not — He set out toward Galilee and the great ministry which there awaited Him. Samaria lay between Judea and Galilee. It would perhaps have been an easier and pleasanter journey for Him to cross the Jordan and proceed northward through Perea. Therefore, the reason that He must needs go through Samaria was not merely geographical. He may have wished to investigate the imprisonment of John and to make contact with some of His followers, as David Smith suggests in his *Commentary on John*. But the main reason was that He might meet the woman of Sychar at Jacob's well and, in His conversation with her, give to the world truths which are eternal.

The fourth chapter of John has been called the greatest passage in the whole field of religious literature. This is because of the evils which are there condemned as well as the great spiritual truths there taught.

When Shalmaneser, King of Assyria, captured Samaria in 722 B.C., he carried away captive so many of its inhabitants that the Ten Tribes disappeared forever from history. In order to repopulate the land he gathered people from five nations and sent them into Samaria. These mixed with the inhabitants remaining and formed a mongrel population whom the people of Judea despised. These people adopted a kind of modified Jewish religion, accepting as authentic only the Pentateuch of the Hebrew Bible. It was literally true that the Jews had no dealings with the Samaritans. When they wished to insult one of their own number they called him a Samaritan. Once they turned upon Jesus and said with suppressed fury and contempt: "Say we not well that thou art a Samaritan and hast a devil?"

Jesus, wearied with His journey, sat down at the well of Jacob to rest while His disciples went away into the village to buy food. While He was resting, the woman of Samaria came to the well to draw water. Jesus courteously and naturally spoke to her and asked for a drink of water. Then began the conversation which Jesus allowed the woman to direct. And everywhere she led the conversation He followed, revealing eternal and saving spiritual truths.

## Evils Which Were Condemned

In the fact of the conversation with the woman, as well as in the content, Jesus condemned four major evils which were then prevalent and which exist still, some of them in even more exaggerated form than they exhibited two thousand years ago.

### Racial Prejudice

The Samaritan woman received the surprise of her life when Jesus spoke to her and even went so far as to ask a favor of her. "How is it that thou, being a Jew, asketh drink of me, which am a woman of Samaria?" If we put these words into a paraphrase of modern speech, they would be something like this: "Well, this is the strangest thing I ever heard of. To think that a Jew like you should ask drink of a Samaritan woman like me!"

Racial prejudice is lodged very deep in human life. Sometimes it is open and violent and used as a political weapon, as in the case of the Nazi persecution of the Jews. At other times it is latent, but evidences of it can easily be found, as in the present relationship between the negroes and whites in the South. But wherever it is, and in whatever form it is found, it is contrary to the principles of Christ's Kingdom and stands condemned by the gospel which He preached and lived.

There is no racial prejudice today that is more deep-seated and virulent than that which the Jews held against the Samaritans. There is no racial chasm which is more difficult to bridge with courtesy, kindness and fair dealing than that which yawned between Jesus and the woman at the well. Jesus set us the example, and the slowness of Christendom to learn this lesson and to follow Jesus in Christian treatment of other races has caused the world and its people untold suffering and bloodshed. Peter early learned the lesson and, in baptizing Cornelius, the Roman centurion, carried forward the work which Jesus began at Sychar. He gives us a record of his change of heart and attitude in these unforgettable words in the tenth chapter of Acts: "Of a truth I perceive that God is no respecter of persons; but in every nation he that feareth him and worketh righteousness is accepted of him." Since God is no respecter of persons, can a Christian ever justify himself in permitting racial prejudice to remain in his life?

## Religious Intolerance

When Ezra returned with his companions from the captivity of Babylon to rebuild the Temple in Jerusalem, he tells us that the people of the land — the Samaritans, whom he called adversaries — came to Zerubbabel and begged to be allowed to help in the work. "Let us build with you," they said (Ezra 4:2), "for we seek your God as you do, and we do sacrifice unto him." This blunt reply was given: "Ye have nothing to do with us to build an house unto our God; but we ourselves together will build into the Lord God of Israel, as King Cyrus, the King of Persia, hath commanded us." Thus the petitioners were treated as heathen having no part in the religion of Israel, and the long period of religious enmity between the two peoples was begun.

The woman at the well was quite ready to argue about the differences between the religion of the Samaritans and the religion of the Jews. "Our fathers worshipped in this mountain [Gerizim]; and ye say, that in Jerusalem is the place where men ought to worship." Jesus did not argue, but in a convincing and understanding way taught the woman the great truths of the everlasting gospel. To her, separated from His own people by centuries of enmity and prejudice, He revealed truths He had withheld from Nicodemus, the great doctor of the law.

The Archbishop of Canterbury, Dr. William Temple, has written that it is not what men think they have found in religion that unites them. This divides them. It is what they have not found, but are seeking. There is none so intolerant as one who thinks he holds in his possession the entire deposit of saving truth. And perhaps none so far from the spirit of Jesus. If we find ourselves intolerant of those who differ with us in doctrine, or in worship, let us remember the words of the saint who said at the end of his life: "I know how little I have gained, how great the unattained!"

## Low Views of Marriage and Family Life

The woman, according to David Smith, was a victim of the working of the marriage law which was then practiced in the Holy Land, and which bore so cruelly on womankind. It permitted a husband to "put away his wife for any cause" and eventually, however often she might remarry, it forced her to earn a livelihood by her shame. Thus the woman of Samaria, being "more sinned against than sinning," was not so much condemned by Jesus in this passage as were the current views and practices of marriage.

The mounting total of divorces in America had become staggering even before the Second World War. The situation is indeed serious, and we need to remember that the breakdown of family life was listed by Gibbons as one of the causes of the fall of Rome. Significantly enough, this was also given by General Giraud in his remarkable published statement in 1943 as one of the causes of the fall of France in 1940. Will America be spared destruction if we do not check the divorce rate in our land, the disintegration of family life which is all too evident, and the low view of marriage which too many of our people, even in the Christian Church, seem to hold?

### Subordinative Position of Women

Not only was the woman at the well surprised that Jesus, a Jew, should speak to her, a Samaritan, but also that Jesus, a man, should speak to her, a woman. The prejudice against women at the time Jesus lived is almost forgotten by those who read the Bible today. Jesus was certainly "flying in the face of convention" when he spoke to this woman, for it was held that a man should not salute a woman in a public place, not even his own wife. Dr. Wescott tells us that one of the things for which men gave thanks in the daily service in the synagogue was that they had not been made women. The pious and self-righteous Jew classed a woman with Samaritans and dogs when he thanked God that he had not been born a dog, a Samaritan, or a woman.

Wherever Christianity has gone throughout the world it has elevated the position of womankind. Women in lands where every right is accorded them that men possess owe an eternal debt of gratitude to Jesus of Nazareth. Never since He sat at the well and talked with the woman of Samaria has there been contempt shown toward women and harsh treatment accorded them in those lands where true Christianity is known and practiced.

## Truths Revealed and Established

As we have seen that there were four great evils forever condemned in this narrative, let us note that there were four great Christian truths revealed and eternally established.

(a) The first of these is universality of worship. In His conversation with the woman, Jesus "wiped both Jerusalem and Gerizim right off the map as exclusive centers of worship." It was not necessary for men to go to Jerusalem to worship any more than it was necessary for them to ascend Mount Gerizim. The great yearning heart of God is continually seeking men and women who shall worship Him in spirit and in truth. It is significant that Jesus said: "For such the Father seeketh to worship him." Even the Jews looked upon

God as a national deity, and certainly the Samaritans did. Now God was revealed as the Father of mankind, and in every nation he that feareth Him and worketh righteousness is accepted of Him.

Perhaps the very fact that we are able to worship God at any time and in any place has caused us to neglect the privilege and to hold lightly what is one of our greatest spiritual possessions. I have wondered what the reaction of the average American congregation would be should there stand at the door of their church an armed body of men who forbade them to enter upon pain of imprisonment or death. Such things have not been uncommon in other countries, and in them worship is now held very precious by the brave souls who believe that they ought to obey God rather than man. It may well be that the Lord has yet some religious persecution in store for us, that we may be taught to value more highly the precious privileges that are ours. Then a church sanctuary seating five hundred people would not be adequate for a congregation of a thousand members, and the vacant pews, which so often dampen the spirit of the congregation and deaden the message of the minister, would be filled with worshipers seeking contact with God.

(b) Jesus also, in this seemingly almost casual conversation, taught the great truth of the spirituality of worship. The only thing that counts with God when we attempt to worship Him is the homage of a devout, humble and contrite spirit. David learned this lesson many centuries before Jesus and cried out: "Thou desirest not sacrifice; thou delightest not in burnt offering. The sacrifices of God are a broken spirit; a broken and a contrite heart, O God, thou wilt not despise." But the people had forgotten David's experience and had made the Temple worship a gorgeous spectacle and a burdensome task.

In our modern, expensive churches, equipped with every convenience and often filled with works of art, we so easily forget that such things are not necessary in worship and even may lure our thoughts away from God. Somewhere I read the confession of a prominent member of a wealthy city church who had come to America from Scotland in his youth. He declared that in his old home church the congregation would meet in an unheated building in the coldest weather and stand while they sang: "Praise God from whom all blessings flow." "Now," he confessed, "in the church to which I belong we sink down into our comfortably cushioned pews and sing: 'Art thou weary, art thou languid?'"

David Smith calls attention to the fact that when Jesus spoke of worshiping God in spirit and in truth, the proper antithesis to truth was not falsehood but symbol, type, shadow. "The difference between Christianity and other religions is not that they are false and it alone is true, but that they are mere yearnings and gropings after God, and it is their realization." After the True Light came into the world, men could put away the futile past and respond to the cleansing, satisfying love and grace of a Heavenly Father, who can be approached immediately and directly. That is our high privilege in worshiping. Through faith we come at once into possession of those things which eye hath not seen nor ear heard, neither have entered the heart of man of the things which God hath prepared for those that love Him.

(c) It was to this poor, sinful woman, as they talked by Jacob's well, that Jesus revealed the truth of His messiahship. Not to the high priest, not to the doctors of the law, not to the Pharisees, not even to Nicodemus did He make known this fact: "I that speak unto thee am he!"

"All the fitness He requireth is to feel our need of Him." So the one who was known far and wide as a sinner received the revelation that was withheld from the religious leaders of the Temple. Surely, there is here something we should give more than passing thought. Those who are self-satisfied, self-righteous and self-sufficient are shut off from the mercy and grace of God by self. "Worship is the submission of all our nature to God. It is the quickening of conscience by His holiness; the nourishment of mind with His truth; the purifying of imagination by His beauty; the opening of the heart to His love; the surrender of the will to His purpose." Self-centeredness is the sin that most effectually hides from our eyes the truth of the saving love of Jesus.

(d) When the disciples returned to Jesus with the food they had purchased in the village and bade Him eat, He replied: "I have meat to eat that ye know not of." In one of the Psalms we read that God gave the people their requests, but sent leanness into their souls. How lean the Christian lives of so many are!

Let us here learn the lesson of soul growth and strength that Jesus gave when He said to the surprised disciples: "My meat is to do the will of him that sent me, and to finish his work." So long as we persist in following our own devices, so long will our souls remain lean and our lives unsatisfied. Only when we yield our wills to Him and crown Him Lord of all do we come into possession of heavenly power and the peace of God that passeth all understanding.

The interview was over. Jesus and His disciples journeyed on into Galilee. Two thousand years have passed, and mankind has never yet caught up with the truths here revealed. But the light is still shining in the darkness, for the darkness has never put it out!

## V

## WILT THOU BE MADE WHOLE?

Two THOUSAND years ago Jesus stood in the midst of a group of sick and hopeless human beings and asked: "Do you want to get well?" Today, great hospitals throughout the land are full of the sick and suffering. Outside the hospitals more are sick and suffering than on the inside. Is there one who reads these words who does not have some ill he wishes healed, some affliction from which he longs to escape?

Can it be that Jesus' power to heal has proven ineffective since He stood that memorable day at the pool of Bethesda in Jerusalem and said to the impotent man: "Take up thy bed and walk?" We can learn a great deal about our own condition and about the possibility of being healed by studying closely this miracle of Jesus recorded in the opening verses of the fifth chapter of John.

Health and "wholth" are synonymous terms. A man may appear strong in body and yet not be healthy-minded. He may give every appearance of being physically healthy and at the same time be soul-sick. When Jesus asked the man at the pool if he was willing to be made whole, He was speaking not only of the man's body but of his whole self. Later we find indisputable proof of the fact that the words of Jesus went beyond the man's body to his inner life, or soul, for the parting admonition given him by the Master was: "Sin no more, lest a worse thing come unto thee."

There are some very important lessons we should learn from the miracle as Jesus performed it before we turn our thoughts to ourselves and our personal ailments.

### The Futility of Looking for Miraculous Cures

The impotent man had been afflicted for thirty-eight years. How long he had lain at the pool is uncertain, but it must have been a very long time. It was believed then that an angel went down into the pool at a certain season and troubled the water; then whoever stepped down first into the water was made whole of whatsoever disease he had. This belief is related just as it was held by the people of that time. There is some doubt whether this explanation of so many people being there was written by John, or inserted by a later copyist. The Revised Version omits it. It must have been true that some such belief was held, or the crowd of sick people would not have gathered at this particular pool.

Perhaps the sick man had tried all the means toward health he knew. His only hope now lay in a miracle, and he had about lost hope, since he had no one to assist him in getting into the pool first after the troubling of the water.

In our own day people still flock to places where they are led to believe miracles of healing are performed. They fall easy victims to charlatans, quacks, fake healers and medicines advertised to cure all and sundry diseases. They follow cults which make health of body the supreme aim of religion, giving up long cherished and precious beliefs, often without knowing that they are doing so. There is a better way to an abundant life than this, and true followers of Christ should never be found among those who would sacrifice all else for recovery of bodily health.

### Willingness Is the First Condition of Healing

If it seems a foolish question that Jesus asked this man when He said: "Do you want to get well?" remember those of your friends who "enjoy poor health." There are people who have fed so long on the attention and sympathy of others that deep down in their hearts they really are unwilling to be well and thus lose what has been so precious to them. It is not at all unusual to find beggars who use their physical affliction as a means of livelihood. These also can be classed with those unwilling to be cured. But when we remember the close connection between health of body and health of soul, we can understand the unwillingness of many to be made whole, since this necessitates giving up the sin they are practicing. Not always is the unwillingness a conscious unwillingness. But an unwillingness which is hidden so deep within a person that he does not suspect its existence is the most serious because it is an insurmountable obstacle to health.

It also may be said that many are willing to get well if they can do so by swallowing pills and powders, but very few are willing to put themselves to the trouble of forming proper habits of eating, sleeping and exercising. Often it takes a complete breakdown to make one willing to do what his doctor tells him, his friends advise him, and he himself knows he ought to do.

### Faith

We are well aware that a sick person must have faith in his doctor if the best results are to be obtained. What we may not realize is that if he who is sick is to be healed, he must also have faith in life, faith in God, and faith in himself as a child of God.

The man at the pool had no faith in anyone, or in anything, until Jesus came. When this man with a strange look of love and power in His eyes, with a voice that reached the depth of one's soul and awakened something slumbering there, said to the man:

"Rise, take up thy bed and walk," a startled look must have come over his face. He had been crippled for thirty-eight years. What foolish thing was he being told to do? "Rise! Walk! Carry your bed!" Such a thing was impossible on the face of it. Yet there was something in this strange man that made the sufferer want to obey. "I can't walk, Lord. You know I can't. But at thy word I will try." Try he did, and immediately he was made whole, took up his bed, and walked.

In a remarkable book, "Release," written by a man who called himself Starr Daily, the experiences of a male nurse in a prison hospital are given. While a prisoner himself, the author found faith in God, in life, and in himself as God's child. It was his joy to help others to such a faith as he ministered to their physical needs. One case he describes was that of a young man who evidently was dying of an ailment not serious enough in itself to cause death. Daily knew that all he could do for the sick man would be useless unless he could awaken faith in his patient's soul. By the power of God working through his own glowing faith, he finally succeeded in restoring the sick man's faith, and the recovery of the patient was a matter of days.

"According to your faith be it done unto you," still sounds in our ears from the lips of the Saviour. And while no one is justified in failing to use all the legitimate means and remedies provided by medicine and surgery and the skill of physicians, after all, it is faith which makes these potent and availing in healing disease.

## No Provision for Relapse

It was not an arbitrary command that Jesus gave when He told the sick man to take up his bed. Obedience to this command signified a complete break with the old life of disease and helplessness and at the same time a firm faith in the permanency of the cure. To make provisions for a relapse in matters spiritual and also, often, in matters physical is to make the relapse easy, if not inevitable.

When a man is healed of a physical infirmity he owes it to himself and to his healer to throw away his pills and powders and to give up his rôle as a hypochondriac. When one is cured of a bad habit there must be no means for continuing that habit left conveniently around. Many years ago a state legislature passed a law forbidding the sale of cigarettes and the giving away of cigarette papers. A college student, whom I knew, filled his overcoat pockets with these papers, stating his intention to quit the smoking habit and to use the papers for tapering off. Before the cigarette papers were exhausted, the law had been repealed, and after a quarter of a century the man was still smoking.

When one has been freed from the power of sin, he must make a complete commitment of his whole self to the new life he has been given, else he will soon find that he is again in the grip of the Evil One. When Jesus met the man whom He had healed, sometime after, in the Temple, He said to him: "Sin no more, lest a worse thing befall thee." No one, whatever may have been his religious experience, can afford to trifle with sin. "Fear not them which kill the body," the Master warns us, "but rather fear him which is able to destroy both soul and body in hell."

The Great Physician is still saying to sick and hopeless men and women the words that opened up a new life to the crippled man at the pool: "Do you want to get well? If you do, if you really want a new life, have faith in God, let the healing streams of life flow from Him to you; rise, take up your bed, and WALK!"

## VI

## DOWN FROM HEAVEN

For the first time in their lives many people in America during the Second World War were compelled to think seriously about food, and where the day's supply could be obtained. Rationing was a great leveling experience, resulting in many things other than the conservation of certain commodities. It went a long way toward bringing the rich and the poor to the same level in the matter of food and thus to a better understanding of each other. It revealed to many their own lack of essential honesty and patriotism, and it showed that much of our boasted superiority to other peoples is more or less a thin veneer that can be easily cracked.

In the sixth chapter of John, we find Jesus dealing both with earthly food and with heavenly food. The miracle of feeding the five thousand is recorded in all four accounts of the gospel and is the only miracle Jesus performed that each gospel writer included in his narrative. This fact indicates both the impression the miracle made on the people and its importance in the life and teaching of Jesus.

## Feeding the Hungry People

When Jesus lifted up His eyes and saw the great crowd following Him, He immediately sensed that they were tired and hungry. Many of them may have come from far distant places to Jerusalem to celebrate the Passover. Few had brought anything to eat, and there was not enough food available in the countryside for so many people.

We remember that John always called the miracles of Jesus "signs." They were not only signs to convince the people of His power and of His Messiahship, but were also signs of His great compassionate spirit. For He entered into every experience with man and was ever sympathetic with human suffering. A messiah without a compassionate spirit would not have been the Messiah whom God had promised and for whom He had been preparing the world until the fulness of time should come.

The preliminary conversation with the disciples, John explains, was not for the purpose of determining Jesus' course of action, for He already knew what He would do. He wished them to realize what their resources were, and how they might be used. Two hundred penny-worth of bread would not be sufficient for everyone to have a little. But when a lad was found with five barley loaves and two small fishes Jesus took the food and said simply: "Make the people sit down." When He had given thanks He gave the food to the disciples, and they distributed it to the multitude. Everyone had enough, and there were twelve basketsful left over — a basket for each of the disciples.

That this was a creative miracle will not be questioned by one who believes that Jesus was what He claimed to be — the Living Bread which came down from heaven. At the same time, the great and encouraging truth of this incident that comes to us, in a day of food shortage and food rationing, is that our need is not too great to be supplied with the resources at hand if we place both ourselves and these resources at the service of the Lord. Has any crop shortage caused hunger throughout the world during our lifetime? Has any great drought or devastating plague destroyed our food supplies? Has anything which could even popularly be called "an act of God" caused us to ration our food? We know that none of these things has occurred, but rather that it was the destructive process of war that brought about shortage of necessary things, produced in such abundance by men when they live at peace with God and their fellow man.

Food for our bodies, both literally and figuratively, comes down from above. God doesn't rain manna upon us as in the days when the Israelites wandered in the wilderness. But He has given us an earth governed by laws of His own making, in which summer and winter, seed time and harvest, do not fail. When men learn to follow Jesus, His example, and His teaching, there will be no food shortages, no rationing.

## *Directing the People to Spiritual Food*

The day after the miracle was performed, the people followed Jesus into Capernaum, where He had gone with the disciples during the night. Their first question to Him was about the way and the time He had made the journey across Lake Galilee. Jesus replied in almost an abrupt manner and not at all as a man pleased by a seeking and excited crowd. The result of the miracle the day before was that the people wished more food and more excitement. Jesus had hoped that some of them would have caught the real meaning and have seen in Him the promised Messiah.

"Verily, verily, I say unto you, ye seek me, not because ye saw the miracles, but because ye did eat of the loaves and were filled." There must have been deep disappointment in the voice of Jesus as He said these words. The people were flocking to Him as a miracle worker, and not as the Messiah who came to suffer and die for His people because of the love He had for them. Their motives were unworthy or "sub-Christian," and if we are honest with ourselves, we must confess that we can find the same kind of motives at work often in the Church and sometimes in our own hearts. The annual Easter parade has just taken place as these words are being written. Churches were filled to overflowing with well-dressed and comfortable people, many of whom were doing no more than patronizing the Lord according to their annual custom.

Perhaps it would have been more appropriate at this service for the minister to have used these significant words of Jesus for a text rather than to preach on the Resurrection: "Labor not for the meat that perisheth, but for that meat which endureth unto everlasting life, which the Son of man shall give unto you."

Jesus is still seeking to direct the thoughts of men away from food that perishes to spiritual food that endures, as He did in Capernaum two thousand years ago. As we think of the desperate condition of men throughout the world it seems that so little has been learned during these centuries. Struggle for power and possessions produced two terrible world wars in less than twenty-five years, and the demons of hell show no sign of ending their fiendish activity.

"What shall we do that we might work the works of God?" was the question the people asked Jesus. What can the Church do, what can Christianity do to free the world from the scourge of war? And Jesus replies, as in the days of old: "This is the work of God, that ye believe on him whom he hath sent." We have tried so many things, and they have all failed. Is it not high time that we realize that just as the people at Capernaum, and elsewhere in Galilee and in Judea, missed the point of His life and message and thus missed His salvation, so have we been missing it by not believing on Him and doing His commands?

*Thou Preparest a Table before Me*

In the section of the chapter in which Jesus seeks to direct the people to Himself as the Bread of Life occur six verses that contain the words "down from heaven."

Verse 33. "For the bread of God is he which cometh down from heaven and giveth life unto the world."

Verse 38. "For I came down from heaven, not to do mine own will, but the will of him that sent me."

Verse 41. "The Jews then murmured at him, because he said, I am the bread which came down from heaven."

Verse 42. "And they said, Is not this Jesus, the son of Joseph, whose father and mother we know? How is it then that he saith, I came down from heaven?"

Verse 51. "I am the living bread which came down from heaven . . ."

Verse 58. "This is that bread which came down from heaven: not as your fathers did eat manna and are dead: he that eateth of this bread shall live forever."

Bread throughout the ages has stood for that which sustains life. But Jesus pointed out to the Jews that their fathers had eaten manna, bread from heaven, and were dead. The bread that He was offering them was of such a kind that they would live forever if they ate of it. He Himself was the Living Bread which had come down from heaven. No wonder the people did not understand what He was talking about. Do we understand any better today?

Much is being written on the relationship of religion and health. Dr. Seward Hiltner, of the Federal Council of Churches, in an important book on this subject, points out that whether an illness is physical or psychic is the wrong question to ask. The real question should be, "To what extent is the illness physical and to what extent psychic?" We are beginning to realize that the whole personality of a man is involved in any given illness and not just the part of his body or mind which seems to be affected.

Under the tension of modern living complete breakdowns in health have become all too common. Whatever we have been taking as "bread," it has not been sufficient to keep men in health, either of mind or body. Many pastors, watching the weakness, the suffering, and the crack-up of so many members, begin to wonder whether they might not have rendered better service if they had studied psychiatry rather than theology!

"Thou preparest a table before," sang the Psalmist in the best-loved Psalm. That table is still prepared. The Living Bread is on the table. It is Christ Himself, with all His healing, life-giving power. This Bread is capable of bringing sufficiency in life here and in the life hereafter. "I am come," said Jesus, "that ye may have life, and that ye may have it more abundantly." But life must be received on His terms, and these are not arbitrary but indispensable and unalterable. If man rejects Christ, he rejects life. In the proportion that he accepts Christ, in that proportion he receives life with an eternal quality, here and now.

## Will Ye Also Go Away?

When Jesus had finished His sermon in the synagogue at Capernaum on the day following the miracle, many of His disciples went back and walked with Him no more. Then Jesus turned sorrowfully to the twelve and said, "Will ye also go away?" It seemed for a moment that His whole life's work hung in the balance, as indeed it did. Then Simon Peter answered Him, "Lord, to whom shall we go? Thou hast the words of eternal life, and we believe and are sure that thou art that Christ, the Son of the living God."

Many who come to the table that has been prepared turn and go away. Jesus follows them with sorrowing eyes, but He cannot change the conditions; He cannot save those who will not be saved.

Let us say that those without the Church are the ones who have been bidden to the feast and have refused or spurned the invitation. Then those who are within the Church are the ones who have accepted the invitation and are set down to meat. But so many of these are not satisfied. So many are not strong. So many actually push back their chairs and leave the banquet hall, having no appetite for the food on the table.

"Will ye also go away?" There are many who are offering ways of life that are hostile to the way Christ offers. "Lord, to whom shall we go?" To those who offer the pleasures of sin? To the weak and beggarly elements of the world? To the rulers of spiritual darkness spread over the earth? There is none to whom we can go, if we leave the Son of man. He alone has the words of eternal life. He alone is the Light that is still shining in darkness. He is the living and life-giving Bread which came down from heaven.

# VII

## WILLING PLUS DOING EQUALS KNOWING

WHO DOES not wish to possess a strong faith in these days when men must live by faith and not by sight, if they really live at all? In His controversy with the Jews in the Temple during the Feast of the Tabernacles, Jesus gave a rule of life which will always produce a strong and satisfying faith if it be followed out. The rule is so simple and yet so profound that its very simplicity has caused it to be neglected, while its profundity has caused it to be too often untried.

Naaman, captain of the host of the King of Syria, in the time of Elisha the prophet, was a great man with his master and honorable, but he was a leper. Hearing from a captive maid of Israel that there lived in that land a prophet of God who might be able to heal his disease, the Syrian nobleman set out with a king's ransom in his possession to interview the prophet. But the man of God would not come out of His house for the interview. Instead, He sent a messenger to tell the great man of Syria to go and wash in the Jordan seven times, after which his flesh would come again, and he would be clean. Naaman was indignant. He had not expected such treatment. He started on his return trip in a great huff, when his servants came and said to him: "My father, if the prophet had bid thee do some great thing, wouldst thou not have done it? How much rather then, when he saith to thee, Wash and be clean? Then went he down and dipped himself seven times in Jordan, according to the saying of the man of God: and his flesh came again like unto the flesh of a little child, and he was clean."

Jesus' prescription for a strong and satisfying faith is found in His words in John 7:17: "If any man willeth to do his will, he shall know of the doctrine, whether it be of God, or whether I speak of myself." R. V.

Perhaps if it should be proclaimed authoritatively from the pulpit of the church in which you worship that one could gain a great faith by climbing to the top of the steeple of the church and there engaging in prayer, many who have never made any serious attempts at obeying the words of Jesus would be ready and eager for the venture. Yet Jesus never ordered nor advised men to do spectacular things. He definitely repudiated the spectacular when He refused to leap from the pinnacle of the Temple during one of the temptations. At the same time, He unceasingly urged men to bring their wills into subjection to Him and to do the things which He commanded. "Why call ye me, Lord, Lord, and do not the things I say unto you?"

## Obedience Is the Cure for Doubt

It was not easy when Jesus was on earth for people to accept the way of life He proclaimed to them. It is not easy, today. So many formerly accepted beliefs have to be given up. So many customary ways of living have to be changed. Even when there is an apparent acceptance, doubts arise in the mind, questions which are apparently unanswerable rise up to trouble the heart, disappointments and sorrows continue to put a strain upon the newly acquired faith. The words of Jesus bring us the assurance we need: "If any man willeth to do his will, he shall know . . ." These words have strengthened the faith of many whose faith was weak. They have brought back to faith many who had lost the faith they had. They are the greatest prescription for the removal of doubt that Scripture contains.

There are many fine and desirable things in life which cannot be obtained by seeking them directly. Happiness is one of these. Faith is another. As one cannot by taking thought add one cubit to his stature, so he cannot increase his happiness or faith by setting out directly to accomplish that end. But, by following the way Jesus proclaims, one can find his way out of any maze of doubt into a clear and satisfying faith, and thence to happiness.

Let us think of some of the things that trouble us in our religious life and then apply Jesus' rule to them.

There are those who doubt the reality of their religion because they have failed to experience the emotion, or the feeling, that they think should be theirs. But nowhere does Jesus set down feeling as a test of faith, nor the lack of it as an indication of God's disfavor. In life it is more often a man's actions which determine his feelings than the reverse. This is especially true in the practice of religion. For example, consider a man who has stopped coming to church. He no longer reads his Bible. He has discontinued his custom of prayer. There is no service to his fellow man, either in the church, or out of it, that he even attempts to render. When asked to explain these actions he replies that he no longer feels toward the church, or toward religion, as he formerly felt. Certainly not! And if he treated his family or his business in the same way he would just as surely lose his interest in them and his feeling for them.

It is a very simple thing, when you attend a church service, to try an experiment on yourself. If you come into the sanctuary and continue talking, if you do not bow your head and close your eyes during prayer, if you take no part in singing, you will experience no feeling of reverence, no matter how carefully the service has been prepared, nor how skillfully it has been conducted. On the other hand, if you come in quietly, bow your head reverently and close your eyes during prayer, and enter into the portion of the service in which the congregation takes part, the proper reverence will be present in your heart without your knowing how it came to be there. It is a wise and rewarding rule of life always to try to feel the emotion you know you ought to feel.

One who makes a serious effort to obey Christ's words about willingness to do His will will never experience much trouble with emotion, or the lack of it.

Again, there are those who have difficulty in accepting the truths of Christianity they cannot completely understand. As a matter of fact, there is nothing in life that a man completely understands. Some of the most familiar and useful things we meet every day are by no means completely understood by those who use them to good advantage — electricity, for example. We smile when we think of Thomas Carlyle's retort when he was told that Margaret Fuller had "accepted the universe": "Gad, she'd better!" And there were many other things that both she and the English sage accepted, else they could not have continued to live at all.

Now, Jesus did not ask His followers to accept the truths He taught in the sense of "swallowing them down." There is a vast difference between credulity and faith. Mark tells us that He ordained twelve that they should be with Him, and that He might send them forth to preach. These accepted Jesus' way of life and acted on it. At Capernaum, when Jesus said to them, after the crowd had rejected His claims and departed: "Will ye also go away?" Simon Peter replied, "Lord, to whom shall we go? Thou hast the words of eternal life, and we believe and are assured [literally, have come to know] that thou art the Christ, the Son of the living God."

In a sermon on "The Laboratory Method of Religion" (see *Modern Sermons by World Scholars*, Vol. 2, page 189, Funk and Wagnalls Company), Dr. Joseph Wilson Cochran describes the return to Christian faith of the brilliant English scholar, George John Romanes. Having been brought up under strict evangelical influences, this man had never questioned the validity of his beliefs until he found himself unable at the university to reconcile the doctrines of the Church with the method and findings of science. Forsaking his faith with bitterness and tears, he attempted in his writings to unseat the faith of others and to show them what dupes they were to believe in religion at all. Years passed, and there came into his hands one day a little volume of science by a missionary in China, named Gulick. This book aroused Romanes' interest, and he wrote the missionary to ask him how he could be a Christian and a scientist at the same time. The answer was that the missionary applied to the field of science exactly the same method he used in the field of religion. He proved all things through personal experience and sought a general truth by studying a large body of particulars. Romanes had never thought of using a "trying out" process in religion. Realizing that he had been working at the wrong end, he determined to seek God by doing what was declared to be His will. Finding the best expression of this will in the life and teachings of Christ, he began earnestly to follow "The Way," letting his beliefs take care of themselves. It was not long until he had worked his way back into a living faith in the Saviour whom he had denied. During the remainder of his life he did all he could to induce men with doubts to give this method a real trial. It is a method that still works.

## Obedience Is the Key to a Strong Satisfying Christian Life

It was not doubts which stood in the way of the Jews at Jerusalem during the memorable feast so much as an unwillingness to give the truth Jesus taught a chance to work in their lives. On the last great day of the feast Jesus stood and cried: "If any man thirst, let him come unto me and drink." He is standing today, "where cross the crowded ways of life," crying out the same words and offering the Water of Life to weary, thirsty men and women. As in the days of long ago, there are still many who will not come, though their experience is unsatisfying and their lives futile. Many Christians would find themselves transformed if they accepted the challenge of Jesus and sought earnestly to "will to do His will."

If it should be asked what was the supreme motive power in the life of Jesus, the answer can be found in His own words: "I came down from heaven, not to do mine own will, but the will of him that sent me." How often He used the words, "I must!" "I must be about my Father's business." "I must work the works of him that sent me." "As Moses lifted up the serpent in the wilderness, even so must the Son of man be lifted up."

Since obedience was so necessary in the life of Jesus, why should we hesitate to recognize its necessity and importance in our own lives. The teachings of Scripture, the accumulated wisdom of the Church through long ages, the experience of strong Christians, all point to obedience to Christ's commands as the one sure way to a satisfying Christian faith.

To the ten lepers who besought His help Jesus said: "Go, wash in the pool of Siloam." And *as they went* they were cleansed.

Jesus accepted God's will for Him as good. And so must we, even though we may be brought so low that we must cry out as did Job: "Though he slay me, yet will I trust [and obey] him." Donald Hankey, who wrote one of the best remembered books of the First World War, *A Student in Arms*, said that religion was betting your life that there was a God. A better religion is betting your life that there is a God *and* that His will for you is always best.

An earnest effort to do His will each day in the little things that life brings would work a change in any man's Christian experience that would both surprise and delight him. We are so indulgent with ourselves, so careless in costly matters, and so negligent in the things from which flow the issues of life. There is not one who cannot make a beginning toward a more satisfying Christian experience, even as he reads these words, if he is ready to take Christ seriously and to begin immediately the doing of His will. After all, it is the little things of life, and not the great experiences, that test our sincerity and the quality of our allegiance to the Master. He that is faithful in that which is least is faithful also in much. If one is faithful in following Christ day by day in the ordinary round of life, he need have no apprehensions about his faithfulness should a great emergency arise, or a severe test confront him.

Recently an officer of my church passed to his eternal reward. At an early age he gave his life to Christ and sought to do His will. The long number of years allotted to him — he was almost ninety-two at his death — brought many sorrows, but also many opportunities of service. He was called upon to give up four small children, and more than fifty years before his death his beloved wife preceded him into the Great Beyond. One son was left. He became the joy and pride of his father's life. During the First World War this son, a gallant captain, lost his life in France. The skies were dark indeed for the father, who was thus left alone from a family of six. But God's grace was sufficient and not for a day did he cease striving to do God's will and to live for the Master in whom he believed, and whom he loved with his whole heart. He became the spiritual leader of his church and the inspiration of its membership. His influence reached out through the Presbytery and into far-distant places throughout the Southland. He became a friend of youth, the stalwart defender of all good causes, the uncompromising foe of sin and evil. His life was full and satisfying. As the infirmities of age limited his activity, his pastor longed for a magic wand to wave over his head and take away fifty years of his age, that he might have that much longer to serve in a place no one else seemed able to fill.

Doubtless there are many other churches where similar examples might be found. But surely, if more Christians accepted Jesus' rule for a strong and satisfying Christian life and experience, such examples would not be exceptional but the rule. In the biography written by his son, Mr. Moody is reported to have been asked one day if he had grace to die. Quickly that man of God replied that he had grace to live and when it came time for him to die he would have grace to die. The grace of obedience, which God gives to every Christian who is willing to receive it, takes away all anxious thought of the morrow. If we do our best to do God's will today, we shall always be prepared for tomorrow, no matter what it brings.

The phenomenal sale of what might be called "Boot-Strap Books," books that profess to tell one how he may lift himself up by his own boot straps into a more efficient, successful and happy life, indicates the profound dissatisfaction with life that so many feel. Like sick people who are always ready to swallow a pill in order to gain health rather than obey the well-known rules of health, so, unhappy and disillusioned people, both in the Church and out of it, seem to be continually seeking some easy and guaranteed way to a better life. "Come unto me, all ye that are weary and heavy laden," says Jesus, "and I will give you rest." And what a rest He gives! What a relief from weariness sinful man finds when he yields his will to Christ and seeks to do those things He commands.

> "Laid on Thine Altar, O my Lord Divine,
> Accept the gift I bring today, for Jesus' sake!
> I have no costly jewel to adorn Thy shrine,
> Nor any far-famed sacrifice to make.
> But here within my trembling hand I bring
> This will of mine, a thing that seemeth small.
> But Thou, O Lord, alone can understand
> How that when I yield Thee this, I yield my all!"

## VIII

## LIGHT AND TRUTH

If it were possible to discuss religious differences more calmly we would discover that those who believe in Christ are not so far apart, after all. Religion, however, comes very close home to people, and when differences of opinion regarding some cherished belief are discussed, usually more heat than light is generated. The result often is, truth which is obscured by heat but is revealed by light is completely lost to sight and old prejudices are more firmly established.

It is a tragedy that so often men tie their Christian faith to certain things which have little or nothing to do with religion. A pastor once told me of a young woman of his congregation who had lost her Christian faith because of the instruction she had received in the biology department of a thoroughly Christian college. She had been taught certain things in Sunday school that could not possibly stand scientific investigation and when she had to give up these beliefs, she gave up Christianity at the same time. Such occurrences have been all too frequent in the Christian Church.

It is well for us to remember the mistakes that have been made in the past, even by great Christian leaders. Galileo was forced by his church to deny that the earth revolved around the sun. John Wesley wrote in his diary that the theory of gravitation was very destructive to spirituality. Jonathan Edwards declared that Christianity must stand or fall by the belief in witchcraft. That the cause of Christ advanced under the ministry of men like these, who were so wrong in some of their beliefs, is explained by what a modern writer has called "The Ministry of Error." As God used Cyrus in the days of old to do His will and to advance His cause, so He has often caused error to render a needed ministry in the Church.

## The Light of the World

The eighth chapter of John, following the section dealing with the woman taken in adultery, which is not a part of the original gospel, continues the controversy between the Pharisees and Jesus at the Feast of Tabernacles. It was a part of the celebration of this feast that the great golden candlesticks in the Court of the Women, also called The Treasury, should be lit. When the attention of the people was thus centered on light, Jesus, seizing the opportunity, stood in the midst of the crowd and cried: "I am the light of the world."

What a stupendous claim this was! It angered the Pharisees, for it was clearly a claim to Messiahship, and at the same time it infringed upon their claim to be "lights" in interpreting the law. They immediately challenged Him and were put to silence by His reply. It would have been wholly in keeping with their dispositions and methods to have seized and imprisoned Him when they were unable to answer His words, but we are told that no man laid hands on Him, for His hour was not yet come.

Jesus is still proclaiming Himself to be the Light of the world. Opposition and anger are still being aroused by this claim. The most notorious modern example of this was found in the Nazi regime in Germany where every effort was made to put out the Light which interfered so seriously with the aims, the methods, and the philosophy of Hitler and his followers. *It's Your Souls We Want* is the title of a book by Stewart Herman, American pastor in Germany, in which is described in detail the effort of the National Socialists to put out the light of Christianity in that nation. But it is the souls of Christian men and women in Germany and elsewhere that the Fuehrer was not able to seize or even to darken. The light is still shining in the darkness, for the darkness has never put it out.

However, it is not in Germany alone that the Light has been hated. Wherever men love darkness rather than light because their deeds are evil, the same thing is true. We are too ready to look across the seas to find regions of darkness. If we looked closer at home we would find large areas of darkness in our own land, and even in our own hearts, areas that are dark because Jesus, the Light of the world, has been excluded from them.

Let us remember that the Pharisees were the best people of their day. There were truly noble men among them, such as Nicodemus, Joseph of Arimathea, Gamaliel. But their minds, as a class, were darkened by bigotry, intolerance, legalism, prejudice and hate. Such things always darken the minds of men, especially when those who possess these qualities are most earnest and zealous. An example is found in Saul of Tarsus, the relentless persecutor of followers of The Way. In his defense before King Agrippa (Acts 26), he says: "I verily thought with myself, that I ought to do many things contrary to the name of Jesus of Nazareth." On the road to Damascus, the Light blinded him physically as he had been blind spiritually. Later the scales fell from his eyes and he received back his physical sight along with an enlightened soul.

Not only are sin and sinful men enemies of the Light, but also men who, possessing many good qualities and traits of character, have closed minds and believe they hold within their accepted formulas of doctrine the whole of divine truth. Surely, it is a sin against the Holy Ghost to refuse entrance into one's heart of more Light as well as to believe that one has captured all the Light there is and thus unconsciously equated one's self with Christ, who is the true Light that lighteth every man.

## Ye Shall Know the Truth

Jesus, who said, "I am the light of the world," also said, "I am the way, the truth, and the life." It is His light that enables men to see the truth and to follow it. Thus, those who believe that they already possess all the light there is, are not even aware of the error that is mixed with the truth they believe.

The words of Jesus: "Ye shall know the truth, and the truth shall make you free," are often quoted out of their context and thus are made to mean something that Jesus did not say. The well-known thirty-second verse of the chapter cannot be separated without grave peril from the little quoted thirty-first verse: "(31) Then said Jesus to those Jews who believed on him, if ye continue in my words, then are ye my disciples indeed; (32) and ye shall know the truth, and the truth shall make you free." There is here no encouragement for believing that truth in the sense of correct and accurate knowledge of a subject will make men free. Such truth does make men free from error, so far as that is concerned, but the freedom of which Jesus speaks is freedom from the bondage of sin.

In the reaction to Jesus' words we find a striking example of spiritual blindness caused by belief that one possesses all the light and by refusing to admit any new or additional light. The Jews exclaimed indignantly: "We be Abraham's seed and were never in bondage to any man." This was said in the face of the fact that politically, they were at the time in the most galling bondage to the Roman Empire; ecclesiastically, they were in bondage to the Sadducees and the high priestly caste, who were in favor with the Romans and had charge of the Temple worship and Temple concessions; spiritually, they were in bondage to the traditions of the elders, who made the law a burden too heavy to be borne.

The "Four Freedoms" enunciated by President Roosevelt, Freedom of Worship, Freedom from Fear, Freedom of Speech, and Freedom from Want, occasioned hope here and among our allies. Posters illustrating them, beautifully done by a well-known contemporary artist, decorated schools, churches and public buildings throughout the country. The "Four Freedoms" stand for a noble ideal which must be realized among the peoples of the earth if any real progress toward permanent peace is ever to be made. But there is another and greater freedom which it is not within the province or power of a political leader to proclaim — Freedom from Sin. "Whosoever committeth sin," said Jesus, "is the bond servant of sin." A sinner may possess all the other freedoms and yet not be free. A servant of sin is held in bondage from which he cannot escape by any efforts of his own. "If the Son therefore shall make you free, ye shall be free indeed."

In these words of Jesus we see the Light that shineth in darkness. In them we learn the truth that makes men free. The Son, who abides in his Father's house forever, has the key to freedom and He only can unlock the prison in which the sinner is confined.

> "He breaks the power of reigning sin,
> He sets the prisoner free.
> His blood can make the foulest clean.
> His blood availed for me!"

## The Service of Jesus Brings True Freedom

The question of human freedom is a very deep and complicated one. Can a man ever be said to be free with all the forces of history, heredity and environment continually playing upon him? Tolstoy, in his famous *War and Peace*, writes twelve hundred pages to prove that men, known and unknown, noble and ignoble, famous and infamous, are mere pawns on the chessboard of life. They are moved, unconsciously but inexorably, by irresistible trends of life and waves of fate. Such a view may seem encouraging at times, but more often it is not only discouraging but deadening. It is certain that Jesus taught no such doctrine as this.

At the other extreme we find the poet Henley crying out:

"I am the master of my fate.
I am the captain of my soul!"

This is a very courageous view of life to take, yet we know in our own hearts, as the poet knew in his heart, that it is not true.

The only satisfactory description of human freedom I know is found in the words of Jesus (John 8:36): "If, therefore, the Son shall make you free, ye shall be free indeed." He alone can free a man from the bondage of sin, and thereafter the service of Christ becomes the highest freedom for that man. It was this freedom He offered the people at the Feast of the Tabernacles. They could scarcely have been said to possess any one of the "Four Freedoms." Yet Jesus did not say anything concerning their external bondage. He struck at the thing that is the cause of all bondage, the removal of which would eventually restore to man every freedom that God intended him to possess. That thing is sin.

It is a disturbing fact that often very good Christians, whose faith in Jesus we would not question, do not give evidence in their lives of being freed from many sins that hinder their usefulness and play havoc with their happiness. Sins of the disposition, such as impatience, intolerance, worry and fear, are prominent among those taskmasters from whose bondage we scarcely seem to expect to be freed. This is the result of not *continuing* in His word. "I am come," said Jesus, "that ye might have life and that ye might have it more abundantly." The abundance comes to us as we abide in Him and His words abide in us. More and more, as we grow in grace and knowledge of our Lord, we shall be freed from all disturbing faults and shortcomings.

In the seventh chapter we learned that obedience is the cure for doubt. Obedience is also the cure for the sins which do so easily beset us. We cannot by taking thought add to our spiritual stature, nor by taking thought free ourselves from besetting sins. But we can do both by a dedication of heart and life, without reservations, to the service of Jesus and to the work of His Kingdom. "How often I would . . . but ye would not," was His yearning cry over Jerusalem. It is ever thus when His followers fail to find complete freedom. The Master is always willing and ready. The disquieting question is, How willing and ready are we?

## IX

## ONE THING I KNOW

If Christianity is subtraction, as so many seem to believe, it is subtraction of the irrelevant, inconsequential things of life, as well as those that are sinful.

The lives of most of us are so cluttered up with a multitude of things that we seem never to have time for much that really counts, often not even time to pause and ask what are the important things.

The words at the head of this chapter came from the lips of the man born blind, after he had been healed of this infirmity by Jesus. He had been put "on the spot" by the enemies of Jesus, who wished to force from him a statement that the one who had healed him was a sinner. But this formerly blind man, who doubtless had been a beggar, would not yield to their pressure and stoutly maintained: "One thing I know, that whereas I was blind, now I see."

After all, it was not necessary or important for a man who had been healed, as he had been, to let himself be drawn into controversy with those who were hostile to Him who had restored his sight. His thoughts and his whole life were filled with the fact of his healing. He could see. Before, he had been blind. Everything else was unimportant. He thus became a "one-thing man," and we can well imagine that the remainder of his life was spent in telling others of his cure and of the wonderful Man who had healed him.

The way Jesus handled the incident, both before and after the healing, showed plainly that He expected His disciples, and us, to learn more from it than that He had power to perform a great miracle. The healing was a parable as well as a miracle. In this one-thing man we find four important effects produced by his contact with Jesus.

## A Concentrated Interest in Life

It is a common complaint that one tries to do too much, too many things, and has too many irons in the fire. The fault is not always with the person, but often is one connected with his position. No organization is more prolific in committees, commissions, conferences, and conventions than the Christian Church. A minister, or a member, who is conscientious soon finds himself so burdened that he scarcely knows which way to turn.

Now, it takes more than one man's decision of will and efforts to change this. We are all tangled in the machinery of getting things done and the red tape of accomplishment. There must be a certain amount of organizational activity, even in a church, but it should not be allowed to usurp the main interests of religion.

When we look outside the church we find a more exaggerated proportion of "busyness" in getting things done. Life is complicated, but we make it more so. There are some organizations that fill a real need. There are many that seem to look around continually to find something to do in order to justify their existence. Many church members have no time for church work because of their outside commitments. Too few seem to have given serious thought to the worth-while things of life.

We know very well from painful experience the concentration of interests that war and its demands make. Women who were already well known for industriousness have found time to give several days a week to

Red Cross work without remuneration. Doubtless many of these would have felt they were too busy with what they were already doing to take on anything else, until war became for them the one thing. Thus they were taught a valuable lesson, and it took a major catastrophe to teach it.

A great experience, especially in religion, makes many outside interests fall away, and concentrates our efforts on the vital things of life.

Lieutenant James C. Whittaker, who was one of Captain Eddie Rickenbacker's companions on the rafts at sea for twenty-one days, wrote, after he had told of their experience and rescue:

"I have told this story as often as I could, to airplane workers, steel workers, shipbuilders — the story of the rafts — and of how during those blazing days out there I found my God. I will tell it again and again, so long as I live. It was the greatest adventure a man can have. It is the greatest story a man can tell."

Every one of us would be happier and better if our interests were more concentrated, and particularly if that concentration were concerned with a real religious experience — an experience of God.

## A Unified Life

The concentration of a man's major interests on one thing will inevitably result in a more unified life. The healing of the blind man led him to believe in Jesus. Jesus found the man after he had been cast out of the synagogue by the vindictive Pharisees and said:

"Dost thou believe on the Son of God?" He answered and said: "Who is he, Lord, that I might believe on him?" And Jesus said to him, "Thou hast both seen him, and he it is that talketh with thee." The man replied: "Lord, I believe." And he worshiped Him.

The difference between a unified life and one that is disorganized may be illustrated by the difference between a vine sprawling over the ground, and one that has been trained to a sturdy and substantial support. Who has not felt at times that his life was all sprawled out without any center or direction — reaching out this way or that, but never rising very high.

A center of integration is necessary for a unified life. Now, that center may not always be a worthy one. It may be positively sinful, yet if it occupies the place of chief loyalty, it will have an integrating effect. The Apostle Paul is a good illustration of a man whose life was first centered about an unworthy aim and later about a most worthy one. He was never a man whose life sprawled. But when we first meet him in Acts he is Saul, the persecutor of the Christians. When the change came, he became just as unified in his life, or more so, as Paul the great missionary to the Gentiles. Like the blind man, he also became a one-thing man. "This one thing I do," he wrote in Philippians, "forgetting those things which are behind, and reaching forth unto those things which are before, I press toward the mark for the prize of the high calling of God in Christ Jesus."

War has the effect of unifying a man's life as it also unifies the life of a nation. The effect of Pearl Harbor on the United States was far different from that planned by the Japanese. Overnight, the nation became unified as it had never been before. Men who had lived selfishly and men who had lived superficially found their lives transformed in a way that amazed them. They willingly and eagerly gave up their pursuits of peace and threw themselves whole-heartedly into the war effort. That unity of men and nation became stronger and deeper with each succeeding month. Without it we could not have made our marvelous accomplishments. And all the disputes, all the controversies, all the strikes, and all the muddling we experienced did not disprove this fact. There were countless numbers who found themselves happier and more satisfied in spite of the privations and sorrows of war.

It is a fact, sad but true, that the good fight of faith has failed to unify the Christian forces of the world and in far too many instances has failed to unify the lives of Christians. This is because we have thought of Christianity as one of the many things in which we are interested and not as our supreme interest. It is true, also, because we have too often postponed a complete commitment until a later and more convenient time that never seems to arrive.

We sometimes speak of a man's vocation without fully realizing that a vocation is a calling and that a calling comes from someone or something outside ourselves. It would go far toward unifying our lives if we held our life work — that to which we are giving our chief and best efforts — as a work to which God has called us. It is not only the preacher who is called to his work. It is every true Christian, and whatever he does to make a living he should do to the glory of God. If he cannot do this he should seek another means of livelihood.

## An Increasing Influence

A man who has had a transforming, or unifying, experience in his life will have an increased and an increasing influence in the lives of his fellow man. We have so little influence over others for good and for God because we have been so little influenced, ourselves. A cold ember can never kindle a fire. A glowing burning ember does so without effort.

Think of the blind man again, of the influence he must have had with his testimony, "One thing I know." Or, think of the Apostle Paul and the marvelous influence this man, small in stature and handicapped by many afflictions, has had over all the succeeding centuries since he lived on earth.

The influence, of course, will be good or bad according to that about which a life is unified. The influence of Adolph Hitler over the peoples of the earth was nothing short of marvelous. However else it may be explained, and it is not so simple as some would make it, one of the reasons is that he was a one-thing man. Believing completely in himself and in his destiny, he became for a brief time the most successful warrior and leader of all history. How near he came to dominating the world we do not like to think. Only the unchangeable plans of an Almighty Power, using apparently broken reeds as His instruments, availed to stop him. Let us not forget this, even while we honor the instruments, as did Churchill when he said of the R.A.F.: "Never did so many owe so much to so few!"

Dr. F. W. Shannon, pastor for many years of a great Presbyterian church in Chicago, tells of visiting the World's Fair in 1892 as a boy. After the passing of years the wonders of the Fair grew dim in his mind, but the influence of a preacher whom he heard there, whose name was Dwight L. Moody, never lost its effect nor lessened its controlling power in his life. Mr. Moody was more nearly a one-thing man than any preacher who has arisen since his time.

When our own influence is negligible, and we grow discouraged in our Christian work, let us look at ourselves and find whether we are trying to persuade others to give first place to that which does not have first place in our own life.

## A Present Salvation

The Church and Christian people have made many mistakes in their understanding and teaching of Christianity, but none has been greater than believing we can be saved only in heaven. Or as some cynic has put it, "We'll all eat pie in the sky by and by."

This attitude of considering life a burden to be borne, the way of life a vale of tears, and happiness existing only in another world has played right into the hands of the adversary, who has used it to retard the spread of Christ's Kingdom.

In one of the *Screwtape Letters*, Uncle Screwtape,

from the regions below, is giving advice to his nephew, Wormwood, and writes about eternity and the future:

"Our business (that is, the business of devils) is to get people away from the Eternal and from the Present. It is far better to make them live in the Future. Biological necessity makes all their passions point in that direction already, so that thought about the Future inflames hope and fear. Also, it is unknown to them, so that in making them think about it we make them think of unrealities. In a word, the Future is, of all things, the thing least like eternity. It is the most completely temporal part of time, for the Past is frozen and no longer flows, and the Present is all lit up with eternal rays. Hence the encouragement we (devils) have given to all those schemes of thought, such as Creative Evolution, Scientific Humanism, or Communism, which fix men's affections on the Future, on the very core of temporality. Hence nearly all vices are rooted in the Future. Gratitude looks to the Past and love to Present; fear, avarice, lust, and ambition look ahead.

"To be sure, the Enemy (which name is given to the Lord) wants men to think of the Future too — just so much as is necessary for now planning the acts of justice or charity which will probably be their duty tomorrow. The duty of planning the morrow's work is today's duty; though its material is borrowed from the Future, the duty, like all duties, is in the Present. This is not straw splitting. He does not want men to give the Future their hearts, to place their treasure in it. We do. His ideal is a man who, having worked all day for the good of posterity (if that is his vocation), washed his mind of the whole subject, commits the issue to Heaven, and returns at once to the patience or gratitude demanded by the moment that is passing over him. But we want a man hag-ridden by the Future

— haunted by visions of an imminent heaven or hell upon earth — ready to break the Enemy's commands in the present, if by so doing we make him think he can attain the one or avert the other — dependent for his faith on the success or failure of schemes whose end he will not live to see. We want a whole race perpetually in pursuit of the rainbow's end, never honest, nor kind, nor happy now, but always using as mere fuel wherewith to heap the altar of the Future every real gift which is offered them in the Present." *

The man born blind, the one-thing man, lived in the present with all its marvelous new experiences. If any man be in Christ Jesus, he is a new creature.

This one thing! What is there that you can hold up as the dominating influence in your life? The central call of Christ to men and women without a controlling purpose, without a great ideal, is:

"Come unto me, all ye that labor and are heavy laden, and I will give you rest. Take my yoke upon you, and learn of me; for I am meek and lowly in heart: and ye shall find rest unto your souls. For my yoke is easy, and my burden is light."

# X

## THE DOOR

CHARLES LAMB once wrote: "Not many sounds in life, and I include all urban and rural sounds, exceed in in-

---

* *Screwtape Letters*, by C. S. Lewis. Used by permission of The Macmillan Company.

terest a knock at the door." When Jesus used the figure of "The Door" to describe Himself, He appealed to the imagination of the people to whom doors and gates meant far more than they mean to us in modern life.

Seven times in the Gospel according to John, Jesus used a striking metaphor to describe Himself and His work. Two of these are in the tenth chapter.

"I am the Bread of life" (6:35).
"I am the Light of the world" (8:12).
"I am the Door" (10:9).
"I am the Good Shepherd" (10:11).
"I am the Resurrection and the Life" (11:25).
"I am the True Vine" (15:1).
"I am the Way, the Truth and the Life" (14:6).

The significance of the words "I am" was not lost on the Pharisees. They readily recognized the claim to deity contained in them, and were infuriated.

There is no passage in the Gospels more comforting and strengthening to hard-pressed men and women than that found here. Whatever else the chapter may teach, the one great recurring theme is that Jesus is Himself the Protector of His sheep and that their eternal life, not only hereafter but now, is safe in His keeping. For "eternal" when applied to life refers far more to the quality of life than to its duration.

## The Door of the Sheep

In the allegory of the Good Shepherd (John does not make use of parables as do the other writers of the gospel accounts) Jesus first speaks of His entering the door as the Shepherd in contrast with the actions of thieves and robbers, who climb up some other way. He then declares that He is Himself the Door through which His sheep enter into the safety of the fold, and from the fold go out to find pasture.

The numerous references in Scripture to sheep and to shepherds are precious to us just because they are found in Scripture and not because they refer to familiar facts in our lives. But it was not so in the days of old. And I do not know what other analogy could so accurately describe the spiritual truths taught in the Shepherd Chapter of Ezekiel (34th), the Shepherd Psalm (23rd), and this Shepherd Chapter of John. Though we no longer have familiar contact with sheep and with shepherds, the figure as it is used in both the Old and New Testaments makes a peculiar appeal to our hearts.

If we should substitute air-raid shelter for fold, it would be more modern but would be a poor analogy, for conditions in a bomb-proof shelter are far from ideal or even comfort. In the fold that Jesus has prepared and where entrance is gained through Him as the door, every need of the sheep is supplied. Now, one may say that conditions in the Church, which through the ages has been the one true fold for the "sheep of his pastures," are far from ideal, and we must acknowledge that this is sadly true. At the same time, it can be pointed out that all the unfavorable things found in the Church have been produced by those on the inside and not by the failure of the Shepherd to make proper provisions. Every real trouble that a church experiences comes from within, from those who are members, or adherents. We cannot blame indifference, strife, divisions, pride, or any of those things that harass a church, upon either the Shepherd, or the provisions He has made in His Church for the well-being of the members. "Let the church be the Church" was the slogan of the Oxford Conference, and it has been resounding in religious circles over the world ever since. But, alas! the church, as we know it, is composed of you and me, and others like us. It is we who make the fold so unattractive at times that those on the outside have no desire to become a part of us.

Surely a transformation would be made in any church if those already on the inside would do their best to make it the Church of God, the Pillar and Ground of the Truth. In these days, when there is so much trouble abroad and men wander about as sheep without a shepherd, what a great contribution every Christian could make, were he to set his heart on transforming the inside of the fold, or the Church, into such an ideal place of refreshment and security that poor, driven human beings would eagerly knock at the door, seeking admission. Thus it could be shown to the world that the light is still shining in the darkness, for the darkness has never put it out.

## The Door to Service

It is also through Christ, the Door, that we go out into the world to serve. Too many members of the

Church — sheep inside the fold — seem to believe that all their concern, all their work should be on the inside of the Church — the fold. Any church that takes stock of its activities will find this to be true. Now, it is right and proper, even necessary, that work on the inside be done, service rendered, and services held. But these should have as the main goal, not the welfare of the members, but rather the preparation of the members to go through the Door — Christ — into the world to find pasture, that is, to find opportunities and places of service. The members are the force, the field is the world.

To come through the door means, according to Dr. William Temple, Archbishop of York, at least three things: "(1) To come to every task and to any part of it in prayer; (2) to refer all activities to the standard of the mind of Christ; (3) to accept what actually happens as nearer to the will of God than our own success would have been. It means putting Christ in the forefront of thought and self, in all its forms, right out of the picture."

How often we have come to religious tasks without prayer, have shown little evidence of the mind of Christ either in our methods, our dispositions or our goals, and have been vastly disappointed if we did not accomplish exactly what we set out to do. Can we not find in these things the real reason for lack of happiness in our lives, lack of influence in the lives of others, and lack of satisfaction in our Christian experience?

So long as a church and its members make it the aim

of their lives to go continually through the Door into service in the world, there will not be much trouble on the inside of the church. I have often watched church organizations search for means and methods of keeping members interested and active. Most of the methods used have to do with the organization itself. And something new is continually being suggested. If fire doesn't fall from heaven, some member always has a match — an idea — to get it started. The best way, the only real way, to stimulate and to increase interest in the Christian life and work is to go through the Door to find pasture — service in the world. And if any organization on the inside of this fold finds that the interest of its members is lagging, there is a sure way to meet the difficulty and solve the problem — let the organization take its mind off itself and, through Christ, center it on the work to be done for Him among those in the world outside.

## The Door to the Hearts of Men

Jesus said: "I am the good shepherd." The word "good" here represents the attractiveness of the Shepherd and all that is connected with Him. A free translation is: "I am the Shepherd, the attractive One." When we go through the Door, we present the attractiveness of Christ to men and to the world.

It is lack of this attractiveness that repels rather than draws men to Christ and the Church. However much those on the inside may be able to see and understand the Shepherd without reference to the unattractiveness of the sheep, those on the outside cannot do so. They see Christ only as they see Him in you and me, who are His followers. The Gospel according to Matthew, Mark, Luke and John is important for us on the inside. The Gospel according to you and to me is what those on the outside read and from it form their judgment of Jesus.

Strictly speaking, there should be no such thing as an unattractive Christian. As a matter of fact, there is much that is bad as well as good in each one of us. We have our ups and downs. In the *Screwtape Letters* it is pointed out that there is a law of undulation in all humans which the devils always take account of. They catch us when we are down. They leap upon us in our ugly moods and try to perpetuate our unpleasant experiences and to make us believe that these are more real and characteristic of life than the times when we are at our best. "In every man," to paraphrase Uncle Screwtape, "there is both malice and kindness. We can't do anything about that, so make it your aim, dear nephew Wormwood, to persuade humans to show their malice to those closest at hand and to direct their kindness to those far away whom they can never reach personally." What devilish wisdom there is in this advice!

Now, if we would show to the world the attractiveness of Christ, the place to begin is right where we are. Let us convince our relatives, our close friends, our fellow church members that we are true followers of the attractive Shepherd, and there will be no great difficulty in convincing those who are farther away. When we sing "Here afford us, Lord, a taste of our everlasting feast," I wonder what we are really expecting. If heaven ever is to come on earth, it must be found first in the relationships of Christians with Christians, relationships that become so beautiful and satisfying that those outside the fold will turn aside to see this great thing.

## The Door to Eternal Safety

Christianity was never meant to be a safety first movement. Certainly, it was not thus with Jesus or with the disciples. It cannot be so with us. But as we labor and serve, as we suffer and wait, it would put iron into our souls if we were always assured of eternal safety and salvation. And that is just what Jesus does for us in this chapter and in this figure. There are no stronger words of assurance in Scripture than these words of Jesus:

"My sheep hear my voice, and I know them, and they follow me. And I give unto them eternal life, and they shall never perish, and no one shall snatch them out of my hand. My Father, who gave them to me, is greater than all, and no one can snatch them from the hand of the Father."

The sheep may suffer and doubtless will suffer. None is exempt from suffering, not even Christ. The sheep may die physically. Jesus died on the Cross. In course of time, all must die. But through all tribulation, and through death itself, they are held secure and safe by the Shepherd, and by the Father, who is greater than all. He gives to them eternal life, life that, in both extent and characteristics, possesses the quality of eternity.

This is not the only place Jesus sought to free His disciples from fear and to fill them with a sense of power and security. In other passages in John we read these comforting words: "In the world ye shall have tribulations, but be of good cheer, I have overcome the world. . . . This is my Father's will, that of all which he hath given me I should lose nothing, but should raise it up again the last day."

Isn't it strange that the followers of heathen religions sometimes live and fight with this sense of security — notably the Japanese — yet we who are Christians and have been given such exceeding great and precious promises lack both the sense of destiny and of security?

There is no doubt of the final outcome of the struggle of right against wrong. There is no doubt of the eternal security of those on the side of right which is the side of Christ. But our security comes not from cowering in the fold as in an air-raid shelter, with bombs dropping all around. It comes from going out of the Door into the world where the danger lies, in company with the Good Shepherd, and doing His work while it is yet day. The Light is still shining in the darkness, and the darkness can never put it out.

"I am the door," said Jesus. When we hear or read these words, let us remember that the Door leads first into the fold, the Church, and then out into the world for service. Only as we go in and out does there come to us that sense of high destiny and eternal safety which we must have if we are to contend victoriously against the demonic forces which are now holding high carnival in the world.

## XI

## RESURRECTION AND LIFE

### A. *The Raising of Lazarus*

DOROTHY SAYERS, who has written religious books of real merit as well as mystery thrillers, wrote a booklet called, *The Greatest Drama Ever Staged*, in which she dealt with Christ's life on earth from a dramatic viewpoint. If we think of His life thus, one of the most thrilling scenes would be that pictured in John 11, where Jesus stands at the tomb of Lazarus and calls him forth from the dead.

#### *Dramatis Personæ*

(a) **The Disciples.**

These were nearing the end of their fellowship with, and personal instruction from, Jesus, but as yet they were very unseasoned and had understood little of what they had seen and heard.

They were still afraid of danger. When Jesus proposed that they go to Judea in answer to the agonizing message of the sisters of Bethany, the disciples said: "Master, the Jews of late sought to stone thee; and goest thou thither again?"

Also, they were still literal-minded. Jesus spoke of

Lazarus being asleep and they said, "Lord, if he sleep, he shall do well." Jesus was then forced to say bluntly, "Lazarus is dead!"

Thomas was ready to "throw up the sponge." His challenge, "Let us also go, that we may die with him," was not born so much of heroic faith as of futile stoicism. "What's the use? We are not getting anywhere. Let's all go and die together."

(b) The Mourners.

Whether hired, or not, these were professional. And professional mourners, hired or voluntary, are about the most trying people those in sorrow have to meet. It was said of a great pastor that he could sit for an hour with a bereaved member and never say a word. Professional mourners are just the opposite.

(c) Pharisees, High Priests, the Sanhedrin.

Among these we find the influential people of that day, the wealthy people, the best people. The word "best" is used relatively. They were the ones who were profiting from conditions as they were, and they did not wish the *status quo* disturbed. "If we let him thus alone, all men will believe on him, and the Romans shall come and take away both our place and nation." In other words, "Let people suffer, die and stay dead, but preserve our place and nation!"

(d) Caiaphas.

He was high priest at the time, son-in-law of Annas, ex-high priest and most influential Sadducee in Jerusalem. Caiaphas was contemptuous of the people, as men in high office too often are. His words to the people after Lazarus was raised were: "Ye know nothing at all, nor consider that it is expedient for us that one man should die for the people, and that the whole nation perish not." A master in the art of crowd psychology, this high priest, who was already determined on Jesus' death but knew the people still favored Him, sought to win them from their admiration by a thrust at their stupidity and an appeal to their cupidity: "You dumb, stupid creatures! Can't you understand that it is better for one man to die, even if he can perform miracles, than for our Temple and nation to be destroyed?"

(e) Mary and Martha.

These were two sisters of a remarkable family, not perfect by any means, but such that they made a home to which Jesus loved to go. What a tribute to a home! How many of our homes are such that Jesus would love to visit them for rest and quiet?

The two sisters represent different types, though perhaps they were not so far apart as we place them in our thoughts. Mary was the quiet, worshipful type. Martha was the extrovert, the activist, the one who placed Sunday dinner ahead of church and Sunday school. But it was Martha who made one of the finest confessions of faith that had been recorded up to that time: "I believe that thou art the Christ, the Son of God, which should come into the world." And Mary was not one to sit and meditate all the time. In the next chapter of John it was she who annointed Jesus' feet with ointment and dried them with her hair.

Mary and Martha make a fine pair, even if there are clashes at times. One needs the other, and neither type is complete in itself.

(f) Lazarus.

In the eleventh and twelfth chapters of John, Lazarus is mentioned by name eleven times. He is the most important member of the cast apart from Christ. Yet, according to the record, he says nothing. Not even one word that he said before his death, or after his resurrection, is recorded. Many legends have sprung up about him. But no revelation of the other world, or of what he did during the time he was dead, was made by him, or written down in the Bible. Paul tells us in II Corinthians 12:4 about his own experience of being taken up into paradise and hearing sacred secrets which no human lips can repeat. It may have been so with Lazarus. At any rate, it is well for us to remember that one can play the second part in a drama and never say a word.

(g) Jesus.

If we had only this one scene of the Greatest Drama, we would have enough to build on for time and eternity. Jesus shows His tender human understanding in the scene; He reveals His oneness with God; He demonstrates His life-giving power; He illustrates what resurrection and life are, here and now. At the same time, we see the conflict in His soul pictured when we read: "He groaned in spirit and was troubled." We see His sympathy in the shortest verse in the Bible: "Jesus wept."

## High Lights of the Scene

(a) Jesus' Meeting with the Sisters.

Martha escaped the professional mourners when she heard Jesus was near and went out to meet Him. It was then that she made her confession about her belief in the resurrection: "I know that he [my brother] shall rise again in the resurrection at the last day." Not being willing to talk with Jesus and leave her sister out, she came to Mary secretly and said: "The Master is come and calleth for thee." What understanding and sisterly sympathy these words contain! The Marthas of the world are always thinking about others. The Marys take themselves too seriously and hence never find real happiness. For happiness comes from thinking of others, not of self.

Mary was followed by her friends when she left the house to meet Jesus. It is the lot of Marys always to have about them too solicitous and too anxious friends. The friends thought she was going to the grave to weep, and that it was their duty to place their arms around her and say, "Now, you must not do that!" It was this misunderstanding of what friendship means, this forcing of one's self into the secret places of another's soul, where privacy should be inviolate, this callous, superficial sympathy that made Jesus groan in spirit and be troubled. Jesus had no chance to talk to Mary alone. Mary had no opportunity of making the confession Martha had already made. Being alone with themselves seems to be a most appalling thing to some people. They will neither let themselves be alone nor permit others to be. And yet it is very true that religion is what a man does with his solitariness.

(b) Jesus Wept.

Only twice in the account of His life do we find that Jesus lost His poise and wept. The other time was when He looked down upon Jerusalem as He was approaching for the so-called Triumphal Entry. Why did Jesus weep here? Many answers have been given. One is that He wept because of the unbelief of the Jews and their thinly veiled hypocrisy. There is truth in this explanation, though not the whole truth. Jesus' inward suffering and troubled spirit were a part of His sacrifice, a part of the price He paid for our salvation.

A quaint explanation is given by David Smith. Quoting from a devout saint of the fifth century, he says: "His tears were caused not because Lazarus was dead, but rather that He must bring him back to the world of sorrow, recalling to the rough billows the mariner who had gone to the peaceful haven."

The reason that comes closest to the truth, perhaps, is that His sympathy was aroused by the helpless and hopeless view of life that even these good sisters of Bethany seemed to have. Although they were friends of Jesus and devout followers, they doubtless were wailing just as the heathen without God might wail. I have often wondered if Christ would not weep again if He should attend in person many funerals in our day, where those who are professing Christians seemingly lose all contact with Him in the presence of physical death.

This weeping of Jesus sets Him apart from all other characters in the drama and all others who have arisen as saviours of the world. Great man that he was, I can't think of John the Baptist weeping. He spoke of laying the axe at the root of the tree and burning the chaff with fire unquenchable.

I think of two elders in a church, whom I knew well. One was stern, unyielding, both righteous and self-righteous. The one thing he harped on was discipline. He was always ready for a trial and apparently for condemnation and punishment. The other was both faithful and gentle. It was not in his conception of Christianity that he should try to condemn a fellow church member. On the other hand, he was always ready to help, ready to point to better things. Seeking naught for himself, he yet gained in the congregation the highest place of affection, confidence and influence that I have ever seen accorded a man. Love made the difference. It always does.

(c) At the Tomb.

If you can picture in your mind Resurrection and Life incarnated, standing before a tomb whose door is closed on a lifeless human body, you may be able to appreciate this scene. It is tremendous in its dramatic possibilities, as well as in its spiritual significance.

Jesus said: "Take ye away the stone." The practical Martha objected that her brother had been dead four days, and that the body was in a state of decomposition. Again, Jesus had to appeal to faith and wait for it to be aroused before He could perform the miracle: "Said I not unto thee, that, if thou wouldest believe, thou shouldest see the glory of God?" The miracle would never have been performed if the sisters had not shown enough faith to order the tomb opened.

The next words of Jesus were a prayer of thanks to God for hearing Him, a prayer of thanks before the miracle had been performed: "Father, I thank thee that thou hast heard me. And I knew that thou hearest me always, but because of the people which stand by I said it, that they may believe that thou hast sent me." This was a concession to the slowness of heart of human beings. Often people still will not believe what they see until it is explained to them. Perhaps they can't, because of their past unbelief. Ever blessed are those who have not seen and yet have believed.

Jesus then cried with a loud voice, "Lazarus, come forth!" The voice was loud on account of the people and not because it required a loud voice for the dead to hear. What a scene this was! The man who had been dead suddenly stood in their midst, bound hand and foot in grave clothes and with his face tightly bound with a napkin. And Jesus said, "Loose him and let him go."

(d) Meeting of the Sanhedrin.

The rulers of the people came together hastily to consider the matter and to decide on action. "What in the world can we do?" they said. "This fellow is performing a lot of miracles. If we let him alone, as we have been doing, everybody will believe in him, then the Romans will come and take our Temple and our nation." Blind leaders of the blind. Having eyes they see not, and ears they hear not. But let us not judge them too harshly, since the highest issues of life and death and of peace and war have been, through the ages, decided by men according to prejudice, self-interest, and the principle that might makes right. I wonder whether, if Jesus had come in this century instead of the first century, He would have met with any better reception.

As we live through the dramatic scene, let us not drain off our righteous indignation in harsh condemnation of the people of two thousand years ago. Rather let us look right around us, where we may find conditions very little better after these centuries of Christian teaching than they were then.

## B. *The Resurrection We Forget*

Perhaps the hardest test of faith we ever face is that of believing in the present and its possibilities. Man ever looks to the past as the Golden Age, or far off into the future for some Utopia, some ideal life, some distant heaven to which he hopes to come.

Strange to say, Christian men and women have the same tendency here that those without Christ show. Yet it was ever the teaching of Jesus, and also of Paul, His chief expositor, that it is the present that contains all the possibilities of good or evil, of heaven or hell. In regard to the Resurrection, it is this present, this "here-and-now" meaning that we seem to have missed altogether. With death and hell all around us in the world, is there anything we need to understand more than the present meaning and significance of the Resurrection?

## I Am Resurrection and Life

It may be difficult to grasp what Jesus meant when He said these words, but it is not at all difficult to understand that He used the present tense. He did not say: "I will be the Resurrection some time in the future." Nor did He say: "I will give this resurrection and life to you as a gracious gift when you die." When Martha said in a sorrowful and accusing voice, "Lord, if thou hadst been here, my brother had not died," Jesus replied, "Your brother shall rise again." Martha then said: "I know that he shall rise again at the resurrection of the last day," and Jesus declared: "I am resurrection and life."

There are six other places in the Gospel of John where Jesus said, "I am," and every one of them referred to what He was at the moment He spoke.

Surely, it is not necessary to take up the statements of present fact that are listed in Chapter 10 in order to show that they were not merely promises of the future. There is a future significance to them, but the chief significance belongs to the present. It was in that sense the people understood Him when He spoke, and it was in that sense that John recorded His words. How can we doubt, then, that when Jesus said: "I am resurrection and life," He was purposely using the present tense? Doubtless it is because we have not completely understood the New Testament teaching concerning the Resurrection.

## Scriptural Teaching

The teachings of the Old Testament on the Resurrection, as on other subjects, was a beginning, a foundation, a scaffolding for the clear and complete teaching of the New Testament. It was Jesus who brought life and immortality to light through the Gospel. Yet we have taken most of our figures of the Resurrection and of heaven from the Old Testament and changed them into facts rather than symbols.

In the prophecy of Ezekiel there is a vivid picture of a valley of dry bones being restored to life when the prophet preached to them. The picture is well done, but it is clearly a picture in which various elements have been overemphasized to bring out needed spiritual truth. So we read that there was thundering and earthquake, and the bones came together, bone to its bone. Next sinews came upon them and flesh came up and skin covered them above, but there was no breath in them. Then the prophet spoke to the wind and the four winds breathed upon the slain, and they lived, and were an exceeding great army.

This was never intended to be a picture of the Resurrection. Indeed, it has no remote reference to the Resurrection but only to the restoration of the children of Israel after their defeat and captivity. But too many people have carried this Old Testament picture over into the New Testament and made it represent an entirely different spiritual truth.

Let us look at the teaching of Paul, who came to know Christ after His Resurrection. He continually speaks of the Resurrection of believers in the past tense. In Colossians 3:1, we find these words: "If ye then be risen with Christ, seek those things that are above." In the preceding chapter he had told the Colossians that they were buried with Christ in baptism and were raised with Him through the faith of the operation of God. This experience to which he referred was something already done. Paul does not always speak of the Resurrection thus, for in the fifteenth chapter of I Corinthians he deals with the Resurrection from the standpoint of the future. But the greater number of his references are to the present.

It is the teaching of both Jesus and Paul that believers, in a very real sense, have already risen again. The true Resurrection is in the present world, in which the sinner, capable of any baseness, rises from the body of death and becomes a redeemed saint capable of blessed fellowship with God. So it was that Jesus said to the sorrowing sisters: "I am resurrection and life." Belief in, and fellowship with, Him cannot be measured or valued in categories of time and sense. Thus a believer rises from earthly into heavenly places in Christ Jesus when he surrenders his life to the Master.

### Life Measured by Quality — Not Quantity

It is still hard for us literal-minded mortals to grasp the fact that eternal life is measured by quality as well as by quantity. And the quality means far more than the length. In fact, Scripture teaches that length as we think of time means nothing at all to God. One day is in His sight as a thousand years, and a thousand years as one day.

There are experiences and stretches of time in our lives that are so precious and profitable they have in them an eternal quality. There are others so utterly barren that they seem to be fit only to be "cast as rubbish to the void." Even when we bear in mind that we may be mistaken in our value judgments, we can see that quality in life always means more than quantity.

Methuselah lived nine hundred and sixty-nine years and died. If he ever did anything with that millennium the Lord allowed him to spend on the earth no record of it was kept and no inkling of it came down to posterity. On the other hand, Jesus lived about thirty-three years, with a public ministry of less than three years, and eternity was packed into that short life!

When individuals are redeemed from selfishness, greed, bitterness, impurity, and malice, they are delivered from the "body of this death," using Paul's phrase. The Resurrection thus becomes a present fact with them, and the length of time they live on earth is of little importance from their standpoint. May this not also be true of nations, for Jesus Himself said that God sent forth His Son into the world to save the world. If this be so, and it is the way I understand the Bible, then every utterance, every act, and even every thought regarding our nation that would separate it from the misery of the world and our duty of ministering to those in need is a denial of our faith in Jesus.

There will be a difference in the other life, but it will not be the difference too many fondly imagine. Peace will be there, but not the peace of inactivity or of emptiness. Rather it will be the peace and joy of consciously receiving grace sufficient for every experience appointed unto us. It will be the capacity and ability to live life to the full, continually, uninterruptedly, throughout eternity. There and then will we have

> "A heart in every thought renewed,
> And full of love divine.
> Holy and right and true and good;
> A copy, Lord, of Thine."

Whatever else may be the nature of the future Resurrection we can be very sure that it will follow the lines of the present Resurrection. "If ye be risen with Christ, seek those things that are above."

## XII

## SONS OF LIGHT

AT THE beginning of the last week of His life Jesus made a final appeal to the Jewish people to become "Sons of Light." It was a yearning appeal, made in deepest earnestness and love: "Yet a little while is the light with you. Walk while ye have the light, lest darkness come upon you: for he that walketh in darkness knoweth not whither he goeth. While ye have the light, believe in the light that ye may become sons of light." Then, John tells us, He did a seemingly strange thing — He departed and did hide Himself from them.

It really was not strange at all that Jesus should now withdraw from the crowd. There were only a few remaining days to His earthly life, and it was necessary that He spend these in intimate association with the little group of disciples — instructing them, comforting them, strengthening them. The revelation of Himself and His Gospel that He set out to make to the world was at an end. From henceforth He will give instruction only to those who have become Sons of Light by reason of their belief in Him.

It is a bit startling at first to note that the word "light," which has been used so often in the first twelve chapters of John, is not used again after Jesus closed His public ministry by withdrawing from the people. The offer of Light and Life has been made to the world. The offer was rejected, as was foretold in the prologue, and only to those who accepted did He give the power to become the sons of God — or the sons of Light.

## The Evidence

From the ministry of Jesus to the people as a whole during the last week of His life John selected three incidents and set them down as evidences of the presence of the Light and indications of what becoming a son of Light meant. The first illustrated, in an unforgettable way, the meaning of personal love and devotion; the second, in an even more striking way, showed the nature of true humility, and the third taught the moral value and spiritual excellence of self-sacrifice.

(a) It was on Saturday, the day before the Triumphal Entry, that a supper was given for Jesus in the home at Bethany He loved so well. Martha served, and Lazarus, who had been raised from the dead, sat at the table with the guests who had been invited. Then Mary took a pound of ointment of spikenard, very costly, and anointed the feet of Jesus, and wiped His feet with her hair; and the house was filled with the odor of the ointment.

This beautiful act of devotion has touched the hearts of men for two thousand years. Yet there were few present who understood it, and at least one, Judas, reacted with a snarl of criticism: "Why was not this ointment sold for three hundred pence and given to the poor?" The explanation is added that he said this, not because he cared for the poor, but because he was a thief, and had the bag, and bare what was put therein. If the ointment had been sold and the money given to him, he would have had an opportunity of getting his unholy hands on it and using it for his personal enjoyment. Men who are dishonest, greedy, and selfish consign themselves to outer darkness and lose their chance of becoming sons of Light. Jesus said little in personal condemnation of Judas. The man condemned himself. But Jesus paid a tender tribute of love and gratitude to Mary for her act of devotion: "Let her alone: against the day of my burying hath she kept this. For the poor always ye have with you; but me ye have not always."

Whenever I hear excuses for lack of faithfulness to Jesus and His Gospel, to the Church and its work, to the Kingdom program of the Son of man, I think of this rebuke of Jesus. How pitiably inadequate will all our excuses appear in the clear, searching light of eternity.

(b) The second incident, showing the nature of true humility, is the entry of Jesus into Jerusalem on Sunday. It is usually called "The Triumphal Entry," but it was probably the saddest day in the earthly life of Jesus. He did not ride into the city as a conquering hero on a charger, but on an ass, the symbol of both humility and of peace. It was thus that Zechariah had prophesied that He should come, yet the people, totally misunderstanding the meaning of the prophecy and the significance of His entry, greeted Him as a man of conquest and war. Their excitement caused them to break branches from the palm trees and strew them in His way and to cry out, "Hosannah: Blessed is the King of Israel that cometh in the name of the Lord!" And these same people, five days later, were shouting just as fervently: "Crucify him, crucify him!"

And still the world glorifies war and might. Until this day, humility is a virtue rarely found and still more rarely valued. It is not strange, but entirely understandable, that Adolph Hitler in his struggle for world supremacy found it necessary to fight Christianity in his own nation as well as in the nations he conquered. For a true son of Light exalts humility and loves peace, and neither of these virtues ever found a place in Nazism.

We are told by one of the evangelists that Jesus entered into Jerusalem and into the Temple; and when He had looked around about upon all things, He went out to Bethany with the twelve. He was too sick at heart to do anything else. His last supreme effort to win the people to His way of salvation was a complete failure, though the Pharisees were beside themselves with apprehension and fear.

(c) The coming of the Greeks with their request: "Sir, we would see Jesus," was the occasion Jesus used for explaining the nature, necessity, and glory of sacrifice. He did not now seem to expect the people to grasp the meaning of what He said, but He must have known that His words would be preserved for future generations, when they could be better understood. There is a scientific accuracy in these words that has been abundantly proven in the centuries following His death: "Except a corn of wheat fall to the ground and die, it abideth alone: but if it die, it bringeth forth much fruit. He that loveth his life shall lose it; and he that hateth his life in this world shall keep it unto life eternal." Dr. Temple, commenting on this verse, says: "Self-love is self-destruction; self-centeredness is sin, and self-love is hell. The soul feeds on itself and so devours itself." Jesus was about to set the supreme example of sacrifice. In being lifted up on the Cross He gained the attention of the world and transmitted to future generations at least the knowledge of His sacrifice and the opportunity of learning its true meaning.

## The Command

Notwithstanding these evidences of Light, the people were still in a critical and unbelieving state of mind. Two final commands were given by the Master before He departed and hid Himself. The first was, "Walk in the light," and the other was, "Believe in the light."

Here was the True Light, available to those who would accept it, and all around was the darkness of this world. The Light was still shining in the darkness, for the darkness could not put it out. But men must walk in that Light, else the darkness that has no effect on light will have a disastrous effect on them. Movement is implied in the word "walk," and all Christian movement has ever been forward. "Arise, let us go hence," are the words Jesus was to use in speaking to His disciples after the night of prayer in the Garden of Gethsemane. As they went forward with Jesus, as they walked in company with Him, they remained in the Light. After them, the darkness was continually and stealthily creeping that it might catch them and cause them to stumble, should they turn aside from the Light.

And how can men, today, be sure they are walking in the Light? Surely, a satisfactory test can be found in examining our lives for love, humility, and sacrifice. If these qualities are lacking, or if the evidence of them is weak, we are in danger. The darkness is gaining on us. Jesus has gone on ahead, and we have lagged behind.

If any church wishes to have a revival that is more than mere emotional excitement or denominational pride, let it set itself to the task of developing love, humility, and sacrifice in its members. If any man wishes to grow in his Christian life and to become more fruitful for his Lord, let him give attention to the development of these Christian virtues in his own heart. They are the best defense against stumbling in darkness. They are the best evidences of one's progress in measuring unto the stature of the fullness of Christ.

The second command Jesus gave was, "Believe in the light." Whatever else this may have meant, I am sure that one of the primary meanings was, commit yourselves to the Light; trust it and make your plans for the future in accordance with your commitment.

There are far too many people in the world — even in the Church — who repeat and subscribe to all the creeds of Christendom they know, without any real commitment. These may even violently profess their faith in an infallible Bible, verbally inspired, but never base their plans and hopes for the future on the development of those qualities of heart and life that make men sons of Light — love, humility, sacrifice. How much controversy, how many divisions, how many mistakes the Church might have been spared if, in this sense, it really believed in the Light.

Outside the Church it is not strange to find the offer of Light treated just as it was treated in the days of Jesus' stay on earth. If the Church does not believe sincerely in the Light, there is indeed cause for despair. But if it does — and it is our faith that God always preserves a saving remnant, the seven thousand who have not bowed the knee to Baal nor kissed his image — then it is our high duty as sons of Light to exert every influence we have, both individually and corporately, to make the qualities of love, humility, and sacrifice recognized and accepted in both individual and national life.

"Believe in the light that ye may become sons of light." An intellectual belief is not enough. The signing of a creed will never make you a son of Light. Belief that goes so deep and is so genuine that it results in the commitment of your life to the Light and its three cardinal virtues, love, humility, and sacrifice, will alone be sufficient.

> "The tumult and the shouting dies,
> The captains and the kings depart;
> Still stands thine ancient sacrifice,
> An humble and a contrite heart:
> Lord God of hosts, be with us yet,
> Lest we forget; lest we forget!"

## XIII

## AND IT WAS NIGHT

THE TRAGIC brevity of this statement lays hold of the imagination of those who read it with understanding. It was night when Jesus met with His little company in the Upper Room. But it was more than night time for Judas when he left the company and went out. He went out from the Light of the world into the spiritual darkness of a night where a man cannot but stumble because he has no light in himself.

The Gospel that has told so much about light now begins to tell about darkness, its nature, its methods, its terrible consequences. Here in the little Upper Room was the True Light. Seated around the Light were now eleven men. Darkness covered the face of the earth. One of their number had committed himself to the darkness. They all feared the unknown things ahead of them. They stayed as close to the Light as they could, but they had not yet been able to understand the Light. He had said, "Let your light so shine before men, that they may see your good works, and glorify your Father which is in heaven," but they had not understood this either. Now Jesus was using the few remaining hours of His earthly life to teach them the things they must know if Light was to continue to shine for them and in them, lest they should just throw up their hands and give themselves over to night, as Judas did, and as far more others have done than we like to think.

## The Way to Darkness

Jesus had said to the Jews in His controversies with them during the Feast of the Tabernacles: "Ye shall seek me and shall not find me. Ye shall seek me, and shall die in your sins: whither I go ye cannot come." He was not pointing them on to darkness, nor was He arbitrarily withdrawing Himself from their reach. He was telling them, frankly and relentlessly, the direction of the path they were taking and its inevitable destination. There was yet time for them to turn and follow the Light. But that time was rapidly passing and the moment would soon come when the opportunity, so far as they were concerned, would be lost forever.

However much we may dislike to think of it, there is truth in the old poem which says:

> "There is a time we know not when,
> A place we know not where,
> That marks the destiny of men
> To glory or despair."

Jesus had drawn that line in the twelfth chapter when He exhorted the people to believe in the Light that they might become sons of Light, and then withdrew and hid Himself from them.

Men sometimes recognize that they are on the brink of some terrible disaster that may yet be averted, and still feel themselves helpless to do more about it than cry out. The trends of habit, of life, of choices voluntarily made carry them forward on their way to destruction, and they find themselves unable to do anything as Christians, or as church members, or as citizens of a great nation to avert it. An almost inevitable accompaniment of such a hopeless and helpless condition is the malice they begin to show one another. Being unable to vent their wrath upon their enemies, they begin to turn it upon their friends, with disastrous results.

There is such a thing as a last moment salvation, a turning to God by a sinner in the face of death, an averting of terrible catastrophe on the part of a nation by actions which reverse the trend to war. But these things at best are infrequent, are not always possible, and certainly are not to be depended on to make up for delinquencies of the past. Therefore, it is most necessary for Christian people to recognize the existence of darkness and that it has its power. Jesus said to those who came to arrest Him in the Garden: "This is your hour, and the hour that belongs to the power of darkness" (Luke 22:53). An easy-going, complacent Christianity in the face of such darkness as crucified Christ and such darkness as has so often made in war a shamble of the world is a denial of all that Christ suffered and taught. It is most important — always so, but more particularly when darkness is widespread and menacing — for us to listen to Jesus as He points His disciples forward through the darkness into the Light.

## The Way Through Darkness to Light

When Jesus told the disciples that He was about to leave them, He used a term of tender affection, found nowhere else in the gospels — "little children." This term must have made a tremendous impression on John, for, years later, when he writes his First Epistle, he makes frequent use of it. The heart of Jesus was touched when He thought of His disciples being without Him and of what they would have to encounter and suffer. Jesus did not say to them that they should seek Him and not be able to find Him. Certainly He did not say that they would die in their sins. Rather, He pointed out that they would find Him in one another. If He could not be found there, He could not be found at all. He had committed Himself and His cause to His disciples. The Light that the darkness cannot put out was placed in the possession of men who could put it out, or who could keep it burning brightly. What a responsibility rested upon them. What a responsibility rests upon Christians today.

(a) Washing One Another's Feet

The act of Jesus in washing His disciples' feet has far more significance for Christians than we ordinarily assign it. Becoming lost in a discussion of whether the command of Jesus to wash one another's feet should be taken literally, we have lost the lesson of true humility that Jesus taught.

The home in which the Last Supper was held was doubtless prosperous enough to have a servant, but the necessity of keeping secret the time and place of this sacred scene prevented a servant being present. Hence, there was no one to perform the customary menial task of washing the feet of the guests when they arrived. The basin, the jar of water and the towel had been provided, but who was to act as the servant? No doubt each disciple wondered if it would be he who would be called on by the Master, and perhaps, eyeing the vessels, stayed as far away from them as possible. Certainly none volunteered, even to render Jesus this service. So the little company sat down to their last meal together, pretending that all was well and as it should be.

During the supper, not before it, Jesus rose, removed His garment, poured water into the basin, took the towel, and began to wash the feet of the disciples. There was no mistaking the rebuke He was administering, and Peter resented it: "Thou shalt never wash my feet!" When Jesus explained that it was necessary for the disciple to be thus humbled by his Master, Peter, still misunderstanding, insisted that Jesus wash not only his feet but also his hands and his head. How patient Jesus was with the spiritual denseness of this impetuous disciple.

The task having been finished, Jesus resumed His seat at the table and inquired of the disciples if they understood the meaning of what He had done. Knowing they had not and not waiting for a reply, He said:

"If I then, your Lord and Master, have washed your feet, ye also ought to wash one another's feet. The servant is not greater than his Lord; neither one that is sent greater than he that sent him. If ye know these things, happy are ye if ye do them."

The way through darkness into light must always begin by the path of humility. The very best exposition of this scene that can be found is in the words of Paul, Philippians 2:5–11:

"Let this mind be in you, which was also in Christ Jesus: who, being in the form of God, thought it not robbery to be equal with God: but made himself of no reputation, and took upon him the form of a servant, and was made in the likeness of men: and being found in fashion as a man, he humbled himself, and became obedient unto death, even the death of the cross. Wherefore God also hath highly exalted him, and given him a name which is above every name: that at the name of Jesus every knee should bow, of things in heaven, and things in earth, and things under the earth; and that every tongue should confess that Jesus Christ is Lord, to the glory of God the Father."

Do we *know* these things after the passing of two thousand years? Do we believe that happiness can come to us only in the way Jesus taught?

(b) The New Commandment

The Old Testament is not without its commandments of love. Jesus said that on the two Old Testament commandments which bid us love God and love our fellow man sincerely hang all the law and the prophets. But this new commandment goes beyond the old commandment. It was the only commandment that Jesus gave. It does not supersede the Ten Commandments, it includes them all. "A new commandment I give unto you, that ye love one another; as I have loved you, that ye also love one another."

If a Christian does not, will not love as his Saviour has commanded, he loses the Saviour. He seeks Him and finds Him not. He consigns himself to the darkness, where he will stumble and may be snuffed out. The new commandment is not one that may be kept or broken without eternal consequences. It is the one commandment that, being kept, guarantees us uninterrupted companionship with Christ. Those of you who have lost your sense of His presence, examine your relationship with your fellow man and it will not take you long to find why.

(c) The Test of Discipleship

We Christians have devised so many tests of orthodoxy. There are always the overzealous and the over-orthodox who want to set up additional tests of their own. But here is the one and only test of discipleship that Jesus ever gave: "By this shall all men know that ye are my disciples, if ye have love one to another." We have had heresy hunters and heresy trials in the Church. But never have I heard of a man even being disciplined for being a heretic according to the standard of Christ. And because we have neglected the one indispensable thing and exalted other things, we have prolonged the darkness of the world and postponed the final coming of the Kingdom of Light.

It is still night for countless multitudes of people in the world. But it need not be night for any who know Jesus. Light can always be generated and shed abroad when men deal with one another in the spirit of humility and love. The members of any church have means available to make their church a veritable lighthouse in the storm and darkness of the world. Wouldn't it be wonderful if all our churches should take Jesus' words seriously and seek Light in the way He pointed out? This Light is still shining in the darkness, and the darkness cannot put it out.

## XIV

## ARISE, LET US GO HENCE

THE ETERNALLY forward movement of Christianity is expressed in the words of Jesus to His disciples at the close of the fourteenth chapter: "Arise, let us go hence." There is to be no turning backward, either here or hereafter, for a follower of Christ. The Christian, the Church, the Kingdom of God must look forward and move forward. This is the glory of Christianity, a glory too often neglected or missed altogether. In the Cross of Christ, God has provided the means for dealing with the past of those who accept the Gospel. He gives them the means of dealing with the present. The future will care for itself, growing inevitably and surely out of the past and present.

With this thought in mind, let us consider the full and complete directions that the Captain of our salvation has given for our safe journey through life.

### The True and Living Way

The opening verses of John 14 have been associated so long in our minds with death that it is hard for one to see that Jesus intended them to be directions for life as we must live it here upon this earth. In his *Readings from The Gospel of John*, Dr. Temple has rendered a great service to the Church in bringing out very clearly the present application of the first four verses. It is Dr. Temple's thesis that "my Father's house" refers to the world in which we live rather than to heaven, and that the picture given is that of a caravan crossing a difficult and dangerous desert. The mansions are inns, or places of rest and refreshment, that await the weary travelers at the end of each day's journey. Jesus goes forward, as a spiritual dragonman, to see that these places are prepared and ready. He then awaits their arrival, welcomes them, and abides with them through the night.

Of course, the picture would not be complete if it should be confined entirely to this world. In a very special sense, Jesus has prepared an eternal resting place for the weary pilgrims of earth when the journey is ended, and will be waiting to receive the faithful into everlasting habitations, into that house not made with hands, eternal in the heavens.

There is not only comfort for each day that we live in this interpretation, but also a challenge. We must never stop our journey forward. We must never think we have arrived. We must face and move forward, day by day, pressing toward the mark for the prize of the high calling of God in Christ Jesus. One who stands still in his Christian life lets Jesus get so far ahead of him that in time his consciousness of Jesus' presence grows dim and his loyalty and devotion to Him become weak. Such a one may sing with a great sigh in his heart the words of a familiar hymn:

> "Where is the blessedness I knew
> When first I saw the Lord?
> Where is the soul's refreshing view
> Of Jesus and His word?"

But these things are not to be regained by going back to anything, nor by beseeching the Holy Spirit to return. Christians are often urged to get back to the Bible, or to return to God. However well-meaning such exhortations may be, they point in the wrong direction. "Arise, let us be going" are the words of Jesus we need to recall, and, keeping our journey straight ahead, we can go forward to God, forward to a new experience of Christ, forward to a perpetual Pentecost.

## Resources Sufficient

It was Thomas, the doubting apostle, who said to Jesus, "Lord, we know not whither thou goest and how can we know the way?" Jesus replied: "I am the way, the truth and the life," or, as Dr. Moffat has it, "I am the real and living way." When we understand these words, we will see the folly of letting our hearts be troubled as we travel the road appointed us, for in Jesus are provided resources sufficient for the journey. He is the only way to the Father and to eternal safety, a way by which the Christian is able to meet and triumph over any difficulty or enemy.

In reply to the request of Philip that they be shown the Father, Jesus proceeds to enlarge upon the resources of the Christian as he travels the Way. He makes the startling statement, "He that hath seen me hath seen the Father," and calls upon the apostles to believe Him for His own sake, or, if they find it hard to do that, to believe Him because of the mighty works they had seen Him do. This is followed by a statement still more startling to the apostles: "Verily, I say unto you, he that believeth on me, the works that I do shall he do also, and greater works than these shall he do." Greater works than were done by the Master? In what sense could this be true of the apostles, and in what sense can it be true of Christians who are living now?

The answer to these questions may be found, first, in the words of Jesus, and, second, in the experience of the apostles and of Christians living in every age since. Jesus said: "I am going to the Father and I will do whatsoever you ask in my name, that the Father may be glorified in the Son" (Moffatt). While Jesus was yet with the apostles in the flesh He was subject to the limitations of the flesh — self-accepted limitations, but very real ones. There were limitations of space, of time, of physical strength, and of other things which may occur to the minds of those who think seriously of this part of the humiliation of Christ. When He went to the Father, His period of humiliation was at an end; wherefore God hath highly exalted Him and given Him a name that is above every name. In His estate of exaltation He is able to hear and answer the prayers of His children, made in His name, and accomplish through them, by His spiritual power, greater things than He was able to do while He was on earth.

When we turn to the triumphant march of the Church from the day of Pentecost down through the centuries, we find that Jesus' words have been fulfilled in Christian experience. The Light that became so dim for a time it seemed about to go out has spread its rays in ever-enlarging circles, until there is no nation or land where its healing power is not known. Darkness still exists and men still stumble because they walk in darkness. But the darkness has not put out the Light and cannot prevent it from shining upon the Way that leads to present and everlasting peace and happiness. Whereas the disciples Jesus made while He was in the flesh were few in number and weak in faith, the disciples made by Him from His vantage point on High, through the testimony of believers and in answer to their prayers, are innumerable and are possessed of a faith that has changed the history of the world, and will continue to change it until at the name of Jesus every knee shall bow and every tongue confess that Jesus Christ is Lord to the glory of God, the Father.

Resources sufficient for each believer as he journeys along the Way have been provided by our Master, as well as resources sufficient for bringing to a triumphant conclusion that portion of the Christian enterprise which has been placed in our hands. "Let not your heart be troubled, neither let it be afraid!"

## Another Helper

The resources that have been named, great as they are, do not tell all that Jesus promised His disciples. He now reveals to them for the first time the fact that another Helper, or Comforter, is ready to come to them in answer to His prayer. "I will pray the Father and he will give you another Comforter, that he may abide with you forever, even the Spirit of truth." *Another* Comforter does not mean One who shall take Jesus' place, but One in addition to Him and His abiding spiritual presence that He has promised will not leave them orphans.

The promised new Helper, who is the Spirit of Truth, or the Holy Spirit, will dwell with the disciples and be in them. His presence will continually guide them in the right direction — forward. He will make known to them, working always from within, whether they are right or wrong in their decisions, choices, words, and works. The touchstone of all their experiences was to be found in their faithfulness in keeping Christ's commandments. Upon this many things would depend:

(a) Keeping His commands was the condition of receiving the Holy Spirit, and in proportion to their faithfulness in this would they be conscious of the blessed influence of this new Helper. "If ye love me, you will keep my commandments and I will pray the Father, and he shall give you another Comforter." The world cannot receive the Comforter, because it seeth Him not, neither knoweth Him, but He shall be manifest to those who keep Christ's commandments, and in proportion to their faithfulness in so doing.

(b) It would be the proof of their love for Christ. "If ye love me ye will keep my commandments." These solemn words of the Master must have sounded over and over in the ears of the apostles as they faced persecution and death after the Ascension of Christ, when the clouds received Him out of their sight. John gives us a glimpse of his own experience when he writes in his First Epistle: "For this is the love of God, that we keep his commandments: and his commandments are not grievous, for whatsoever is born of God overcomes the world." They are words that should never be absent from our hearts and minds. Obedience is the proof of our love for Christ, and from obedience comes power to overcome the world.

(c) It would also be the source of peace. Only in keeping Christ's commands were the disciples to find peace. "These things have I spoken unto you, being yet present with you. The Comforter shall teach you all things and bring all things to your remembrance, whatsoever I have said unto you. Peace I leave with you, my peace I give unto you. Not as the world giveth, give I unto you." Peace for the disciples was inseparably connected with obedience to the Master's commands. Peace for the Christian today is still found in obedience and found only there. For, as Studdert-Kennedy has truly written:

> "Peace doest not mean the end of all our striving,
> Joy does not mean the drying of our tears,
> Peace is the power that comes to souls arriving
> Up to that light where God alone appears!"

Keeping the commands of Christ is too much to ask of any mortal man who is dependent upon his own resources. It was too much to ask of the apostles, even though they had spent three years in company with Jesus. But it is not too much to ask of the most humble Christian who understands the work and mission of the Holy Spirit, and, with this Helper at his side and within him, sets out to follow the true and living Way. For such a one, safe passage all along the journey of life through this world is guaranteed by Him who is Himself the Way, the Truth and the Life.

Wherever there is a Christian who is weary, discouraged, and afraid, let him hearken to the words of Jesus as He gives orders to advance: "Arise, let us go hence!" Is there a church that seems to have reached the end of its usefulness and service and is ready to give up and close its doors? The orders are the same, and the remedy for fruitlessness is contained in them: "Launch out into the deep! Forward with Christ! Arise, let us go hence!" The Light is still shining in the darkness. The Way ahead is clear, unmistakable, and glorious, a way to Victory and Peace.

## XV

## YE ARE MY FRIENDS, IF —

THERE IS an ancient legend that a king's son had three friends, or three intimate associates whom he thought were his friends. The first he loved better than he loved himself, the second, as well, and the third, less. At his father's suggestion, he put their friendship to the test. Pretending to have accidentally killed a man and to have been sentenced therefor to crucifixion, he asked these friends what assistance they could give him. The first coolly offered the needful cloth for wrapping his dead body, the second, more tenderly, expressed a willingness to be near him to the end and to console him, but the third was prompt and earnest to say that he would die for him if he could, or else he would die with him.

Before Jesus told His little group of disciples the conditions they must fulfill if they were to be His friends He said: "Greater love hath no man than this, that a man lay down his life for his friends." Then He added: "Ye are my friends if ye do whatsoever I command you. Henceforth I call you not servants; for the servant knoweth not what his lord doeth: but I have called you friends; for all things that I have heard of my Father I have made known unto you."

Dr. Henry Clay Trumbull, the great pioneer Sunday-school leader, gave one of the many books he wrote the title, *Friendship, The Master Passion*. As he presents material gathered from past ages illustrating the influence of friendship in the lives of men, he seems to establish his thesis that friendship is the master passion of life and inspires men to noblest actions. When Charles Kingsley was asked to account for his rich life, he said simply, "I had a friend." Everyone who has entered into the soul-satisfying beauty of a true friendship can say with the poet:

"God never blessed me in so sweet a way before;
'Tis He alone who can such blessings send:
For when He would His fullest love declare,
He brought thee to me, saying, 'Behold a friend!'"

It is significant that Jesus did not make the statement, "I am your friend if ye do whatsoever I command you," but rather, "Ye are my friends if you do whatsoever I command you." When Jesus calls men friends, as He called the disciples, they are placed under the highest obligation to fulfill the conditions of friendship that He lays down. He forever proved and established His love for men by sacrificing His life in their behalf. His part of friendship's conditions have been met and the results are unchangeable. The disciples must henceforth meet their part of the conditions lest they lose the supreme opportunity of possessing in life a Friend who will satisfy their every need.

The conditions of an uninterrupted and increasingly satisfying friendship with Jesus are given us in this fifteenth chapter of John.

## Abide in Me and I in You

The first condition is that we must remain united to Him so that He may remain united to us.

There was a golden vine on the porch of Herod's temple, through which Jesus and the disciples passed on their way from the Upper Room to the Garden of Gethsemane. This was doubtless the immediate occasion of the allegory of the vine and the branch with which the chapter begins. Israel had been known for centuries as the "vine of God's own planting." But Israel had not brought forth fruit. "The Lord looked that it should bring forth grapes, and it brought forth wild grapes." (Isaiah 5:2.) Now Jesus proclaims Himself to be the true Vine and those who believe in Him are the branches. In the life of the vegetable kingdom, branches have no choice about remaining united to the vine. They may be severed from the vine by some outside force, but they do not and cannot sever themselves. The figure, therefore, does not represent perfectly the relationship of Christ and His followers, but it illustrates in an unforgettable way the necessity for Christians in every age to remain united to Him as branches remain united to a vine.

Friendship requires constant attention if it is to be preserved and strengthened. It will not grow, nor even live, if it is neglected. There are few real friendships among us because we are so exceedingly busy here and there we do not seem to have time for cultivating friends. At his death, it was said in appreciation of Dr. Frank Gunsaulus, founder of Armour Technical Institute, that he had a talent for living and a genius for friendship. This is an indication of true greatness. But talent and genius always depend more on what we do with them than on the original endowment. Dr. Gunsaulus cultivated his friends. Everyone, with or without genius, must also do this if he is to have friends and enjoy friendship.

If we are to remain Jesus' friends, according to His words, we must abide in Him and He in us. This is not an arbitrary requirement that He set up. It is a necessary condition according to the very nature of friendship. If we are to remain His friends we must stay close to our Friend in spirit.

Friendships in life are made stronger by attention to little things that seem of no great importance at the time, but turn out to be of eternal significance. Conversely, friendships are weakened by neglect, forgetfulness, and indifference. There are certain things that the Church in its centuries of experience has found to be valuable in keeping believers closely united with Christ and thus keeping this priceless friendship intact. The Church magnifies these things and too often we set our individual wisdom against that of the Church and our self-interests against that which the Church declares must be done in the interests of our souls. It is highly important that we make diligent use of the means of grace Christ placed at our disposal when He founded the Church if we wish to be friends with whom He is pleased.

To "abide in Christ," we must "practice His presence," read the Holy Scriptures regularly, establish and continue the habit of daily prayer, attend the public services of worship of our church, and partake of the Holy Sacraments. If these things are done in spirit and in truth, humbly and with loving hearts, we necessarily grow in grace and in the knowledge of our Lord and Saviour. We abide in Him and He in us. We keep cultivated the precious flower of friendship with Jesus.

## Bringing Forth Fruit

The second condition of friendship with our Saviour is fruit-bearing. The Father, who is the husbandman, or vine dresser, cuts away unfruitful branches. Being severed from the vine and useless, men gather the cut branches and cast them into the fire, and they are burned. Branches that bear fruit are pruned by the vine dresser so that they may bring forth more fruit, for bearing much fruit glorifies the Father.

Bearing fruit is presented by the Master as a duty rather than a privilege of discipleship. It is a privilege, but it is first a duty and one that is neglected at the peril of losing all connection with the vine. The average Christian seems not to understand the warning of peril that is here given. There are those who have been Christians for years but show no evidence of bearing fruit in their lives. There must be some fruit somewhere, else they would have been cut off as branches. But there is not enough to keep their friendship with Jesus strong and satisfying, and not enough to glorify God.

Anything that interferes with fruit-bearing in the Christian must be cut away. This pruning process hurts and sometimes cuts into those things that we had thought were our best works. Unless these favorite and best works of ours produce fruit, they are of no use to the Lord and of no value in the Church. Now, however necessary "winning souls" may be, the reference here is not to that kind of fruit. "The fruit of the spirit," wrote Paul to the Galatians, "is love, joy, peace, long suffering, gentleness, goodness, faith, meekness, temperance." It is this kind of fruit that Jesus expects His disciples to bear as they abide in Him as branches in a vine. And it is this kind of fruit that is often conspicuously lacking in highly successful churches where members are received weekly by the score or hundreds, and souls are being saved in such numbers as to arouse the envy of sister churches.

When one finds that his zeal in Christian work and service is interfering with real fruit-bearing in his life, the message of a little poem by Caroline Tickner may help to set things in his life in a better perspective:

> "With calm brave purpose every day renew,
> And let each moment planned and precious be,
> And thou shalt find thou hast just time to do
> What God requires of thee.
>
> "What God requires, who knoweth well thy frame,
> Not what thy friends or those around may ask;
> The ceaseless bustle and the over-strain,
> Of self-imposed task.
>
> "Be not of careless or of anxious mind,
> But let His gracious peace thy spirit fill
> With quiet diligence to seek and find
> Just time to do His will."

### Loving One Another

All the way through this chapter, three things are joined as a kind of inseparable trilogy: obedience, abiding in Christ and in His love, loving one another. The words, "Ye are my friends if ye do whatsoever I have commanded you," are preceded by the statement: "This is my commandment, that ye love one another as I have loved you." This is the New Commandment that He gave His disciples, the supreme condition of friendship with Him that must be fulfilled lest all else we do be in vain. Yet, if we are entirely honest with ourselves, we will have to confess that it is here we fail most often, and even seem to make very little effort to obey this commandment.

The lack of love, one for the other, that Jesus saw

daily among the little group that followed Him must have burdened His heart. Time and again, He rebuked them for their selfishness, their personal ambition, their quarrelling among themselves. It is as if He said to them: "If ye do not learn to love one another and to treat each other with brotherly affection, there is no use in your going out into the world with the message of salvation." The very credentials of discipleship that they were to show to the world were to be the love they had for one another: "By this shall all men know that ye are my disciples, if ye have love one for the other." In his First Epistle, John wrote that this should be their own assurance of salvation: "We know that we have passed from death unto life because we love the brethren."

How well the disciples learned this lesson, and how faithfully they put into practice the command, can be seen from the surprised exclamation of their persecutors, that has come down to us: "Behold, how these Christians love one another!"

When we begin to examine our own relationships with our fellow Christians, and discover the lack of love in our hearts, we will understand perhaps why we have not made more progress in our friendship with Christ. Dr. Charles E. Jefferson wrote in *The Building of the Church* that the members of the city church do not know each other and do not want to, whereas the members of the country church do know each other and are sorry they do. This charge is perhaps an exaggeration, but it puts in a startling way the lack of real Christian love that exists in many congregations.

When we remember that Jesus commanded His followers to love their enemies, we must realize that love among the brethren is a *sine qua non* of Christian discipleship. But, just as no man by taking thought can add one cubit to his stature, so no man by mere force of the will can make himself love his fellow man. How then should one deal with himself and his lack of brotherly love? John must have thought much on this subject, for he works out the answer in detail in his First Epistle. "God is love, and he that dwelleth in love dwelleth in God, and God in him. We love because he first loved us." Just as it is impossible for believers to remain united with Christ if they do not love each other, so it is a natural, not to say an inevitable, result of abiding in Christ to love one another. One cannot abide in love and be immune to love. One cannot maintain an intimate, vital connection with the Source of all love and not be progressively filled with love, himself. It is thus the one sure test of our friendship with Christ, that we love one another, for apart from Christ the love of self is the predominant quality of the human heart.

"Toward the end of his life [according to Jerome, quoted by Plummer in the Cambridge Greek Testament] the aged Apostle John was so infirm that he had to be carried to church and was too weak to preach. He used often to say no more than this, 'Little children, love one another.' His hearers at last wearied of this, and said: 'Master, why dost thou always say this?' 'It is the Lord's command,' he replied, 'and if this alone is done, it is enough.' "

"This commandment have we from him, that he who loveth God loveth his brother also."

The disciples were not promised immunity from suffering and persecution by the Master as He bade them farewell. Instead, they were warned that the same type of persecution awaited them that they had witnessed their Master suffer. But they were promised His friendship and, with such a Friend, they were sufficient for every experience of life. The promise is the same for Christians in our day, as in the days of long ago: "Ye are my friends, if — " Are you meeting the conditions of friendship with Jesus?

## XVI

## OVERCOMING THE WORLD

When a man is forewarned of trouble and given the means of forearming himself, he is indeed hopeless if, through neglect or choice, he fails to use the means.

Jesus was giving the disciples His last intimate and soul-searching talk. He had done all He could for them. Their safety and salvation, and that of future generations, now depended on how well they understood His words and how faithfully they followed His instructions. There comes a time in the experience of every one when not even the Lord can do any more for him. He must do for himself, with the means God has provided, else he will never come into the Light, but will consign himself to outer darkness. Thank

God, the disciples used the means, however imperfectly this may have been done at first. Thank God, men can do the same, today, and by using them are able to overcome the world.

## In the World — Trouble

The statement, "In the world ye have trouble," that Jesus made to His disciples has proven true for every generation of men since, and for every individual. To accept this fact is to begin to deal with it wisely. To imagine one's self an exception and then to resist and resent trouble is to bring sorrow upon sorrow.

No one seeks or desires trouble. Certainly the disciples did not. But in a world where sin and death are at work, it is impossible to escape it. Jesus used this common but telling illustration of the relation of sorrow and trouble to joy: "A woman when she is in travail hath sorrow, because her hour is come: but when she is delivered of the child, she remembereth no more the anguish, for the joy that a man is born into the world." There is no better illustration of joy out of sorrow for us to carry in our hearts as we suffer in this world of sin than this one that Jesus Himself gave.

Sadly enough, there are many Christians who have never accepted the fact of trouble and sorrow in this world and who make themselves and those who love them miserable because of their unchristian reactions. The attitude expressed in the words, "Why did God do this to me?" when trouble and sorrow come is most piteous, futile, and unchristian. God had one Son without sin, but no Son without suffering; and the disciple is not above his Lord, nor he that is sent above Him that sent him.

If men and women had not been afflicted by sin, God would not have sent His Son into the world to save them. If one should be free from all afflictions now he would not feel his need of a Saviour. "Whom the Lord loveth he chasteneth, and scourgeth every son whom he receiveth." And chastening still seemeth for the present to be not joyous but grievous; yet afterward it still yieldeth peaceable fruit to them that are trained by it.

## In Christ — Peace

Jesus had preceded His warning to the disciples of trouble and sorrow in the world with the comforting promise that in Him they were able to have peace. "These things have I spoken unto you, that in me ye may have peace." He was referring to all that He had spoken to them since they had entered the Upper Room, but more particularly to what He had just told them of His relationship to the Father, and of the mission of the Holy Spirit.

The Master Himself always had peace, because He was one with the Father and because He had the Holy Spirit without measure. Peace came to Him from within and was utterly independent of things without. Wherever we find Jesus, whatever the outward circumstances were, He was possessed of an inward, regnant peace that enabled Him to tower above all His enemies and all their power. They could break His body, even break His heart, but they could not break His peace.

The Apostle Paul, with a clear understanding of these words of Jesus, wrote an expansion of them in Philippians 4:6: "In nothing be anxious; but in everything by prayer and supplication with thanksgiving let your requests be known unto God. And the peace of God which passeth all understanding shall guard your hearts and your thoughts in Christ Jesus." — R. V. In Christ, we can have the peace of God to stand as a sentinel at the door of the inner citadel of our hearts.

There is in these words of Jesus and of Paul, a reference to prayer and, particularly, to prayer of petition, or asking. "If ye shall ask anything of the Father, He will give it to you in my name. Hitherto have ye asked nothing in my name: ask and ye shall receive that your joy may be made full." The disciples had not prayed in the name of Jesus up to this time because He was still with them, but more particularly because they did not know what asking in the name of Jesus meant. There are too many mature Christians who still think that asking in the name of Jesus means merely appending the phrase, "For Christ's sake," to the end of their prayers as a kind of magic formula. It is well to end our prayers with these words for they keep us reminded that God hears us because of the merits of His Son. But many prayers are not made in the name of Christ even though the words are used, and some prayers may be in His name without their being used at all. Prayer in the name of Christ is prayer offered in His spirit of love and humility for those things that are in accordance with

His character, and that promote His cause and kingdom in the world and in the hearts of men.

In the world, trouble; in Christ, peace! How truly did Jesus see and understand what lay in front of His followers down through the centuries. And how unerringly did He point out to them the things that belonged to their peace. For peace is not the ultimate goal of our struggles in the Christian life. Rather it is the armament of spirit the Christian may possess as he follows the example of his Master in overcoming the world.

### The Means toward the End — The Holy Spirit

Strange, indeed, in the ears of the little apostolic group must have sounded the words of Jesus when He said: "It is expedient for you [that is, for your good] that I go away."

They were timid and fearful in the presence of their enemies, clinging to Him as little children to a parent when danger threatens. But their strength must come, if ever, from within them and not from anything without, even though it be the personal presence of Jesus. And Jesus hastens to explain that when He leaves them He will send them the Comforter, or the Helper, who shall work within their hearts.

In this sixteenth chapter of John more is said in explanation of the mission and work of the Holy Spirit than in any other passage in the New Testament. The explanation is practical rather than theological, and should be understood by every Christian who desires to be a true follower of Jesus in overcoming the world.

The work of the Holy Spirit in the world is a work of conviction, and not always, nor necessarily, a saving conviction. The world must and will be convicted of sin, of righteousness, and of judgment.

(a) Of sin — the sin of the rejection and crucifixion of Christ. "This is ever the damning sin — to be in the presence of goodness and not to love it, to see Christ and to see Him with unmoved and unloving hearts, to hear His call without response, to recognize the beauty of holiness and yet turn away to lust, and self, and the world."

(b) Of righteousness. When conscience ceases to condemn, hope dies. This conviction is that there is such a thing as righteousness but that it is unattainable by any means the world has at its disposal. Righteousness, which is right living and right relationship with God and man, can be had only through belief in, and acceptance of, Christ and His gospel.

(c) Of judgment. Jesus' statement that the prince of this world hath been judged must be a matter of faith until experience shows it to be true. His doom is sealed, and the fate of those who are doing his bidding will, one by one, confirm the faith of Christians, and strengthen the conviction of the world that nothing apart from, or contrary to, Christ and His cause can stand. When the rains, the floods and the winds of judgment come, every house not built upon the Rock must fall. Satan still carries on his hopeless work but his doom is sure, and that of all his followers.

The work of the Holy Spirit in the heart of believers is a different and a saving work. He guides them into all truth in Christ, for He is the Spirit of Truth. He makes it possible for a Christian to abide in Christ and for Christ's words to abide in the Christian's heart. He gives the inner force and power that each must have if he is to overcome the world. He cleanses the heart, strengthens the will and clears the mind so that everyone in whom He dwells may be, like Christ, independent of outward things and possessed of inner resources the world knows nothing about, cannot understand and is utterly unable to resist. Thus it was good for the apostles that Christ should go away and that the Holy Spirit should come. The Day of Pentecost marked the beginning of the distinctive work of the Spirit, a work that shall continue until victory over the world is finally and completely won.

The evidence of the presence and power of the Holy Spirit in the Church, and in believers, is not to be found in strange and bizarre experiences, as too many have vainly imagined. Rather, we can be very sure that the Spirit is at work in a man's heart when he gives evidence of becoming more Christ-like in his relations with his fellow man and more faithful in his performance of Christian duties. A Church shows the gracious work of the Spirit when its members begin to love one another as Jesus loves them, taking seriously the New Commandment He gave the disciples and remembering that the only test for orthodoxy our Saviour proposed was the test of love. These things seem to have been very hard for the Church to understand, and down through the centuries other standards of orthodoxy have been set up and other evidences of spiritual power have been accepted as more real.

The words of Jesus to the disciples: "Be of good cheer, I have overcome the world," fall upon our ears with soothing, sustaining power, just as they must have fallen on the ears of the disciples. We know that He overcame the world. The evidence of this is so plentiful and plain that only those whose eyes are blinded by sin fail to see it. He who has overcome the world will not suffer the world to overcome His disciples. Confidence in our Leader, loyalty to His plan of salvation, faithfulness in carrying out His program, these are the things that enable Christian men and women to be more than conquerors in all life's experiences, through Him that loveth us.

The Light is still shining in the darkness, for the darkness has never put it out.

## XVII

## JESUS' PRAYER FOR PEACE

ALL THE finest efforts of men toward establishing peace on earth have proved to be failures. At best, these efforts can only be said to have been unavailing. At the worst, they may have been altogether wrong. We have thought in terms of the disease. We have denounced war and many brave souls, believing they were doing the very best they could, have declared they would never again bless a war and would have nothing to do with the war system. But the effort to banish war from the earth by denouncing it is comparable to an effort to banish a disease like smallpox by denouncing smallpox and declaring that we will have nothing to do with it. Disease pays no attention to denunciation, and neither does war. The cause of the disease must be found, the man who is afflicted must be treated, and the means to prevent its spread must be found, else all our horror, loathing and hatred of the disease will be without effect.

In the seventeenth chapter of John, we see and hear Jesus at prayer. It is the only complete prayer of the Master that the Scriptures contain. It is the true Lord's prayer, for the prayer in the sixth chapter of Matthew, commonly called the Lord's Prayer, could never have been used as a prayer by our Saviour and should be called the Disciples' prayer. There is no passage in Holy Writ that is quite so sacred as this prayer of Jesus, and none that so deeply touches the hearts of men. Yet we have largely missed its real meaning and thus have missed its benefits in our lives, because of slowness of heart to understand, to believe, and to live according to its petitions.

## The Prayer

The Lord's prayer is divided into three parts. Jesus prays first for Himself, then for His disciples and then for believers in every age of the history of the world.

(a) The petitions that Jesus makes for Himself are found in the first five verses. He lifted up His eyes to heaven, declared that the hour was come and prayed that God would glorify the Son so that the Son might glorify the Father. It was the hour for manifesting to the world the glory He had with the Father before the world existed, a glory He had voluntarily surrendered when He was born into the world that He might gain it again in giving eternal life to those who believed in Him. This work was now finished, so far as His part of it, as the God-man, was concerned.

(b) Beginning with the sixth verse, Jesus prays for His disciples. He had done all He could for them. He had revealed God's real self to them, had made known to them all they needed to know about God, had kept and protected them and, as both priest and victim, had purified Himself for His sacrificial offering on their behalf. The burden of this portion of the prayer was that the disciples should be one, as He was one with God and should be kept from the evil one. They were not to be taken out of the world, but being sanctified, or purified, through the truth and thus being out of reach of the evil things of life, were to be sent out into the world with the same message of redemption Jesus brought from heaven to earth.

(c) At the twentieth verse, the prayer leaps forward through the succeeding days and years and centuries, and includes in its petitions all who believe and accept the gospel. In this portion of the prayer, where you and I, with our spiritual needs, are presented to the Father for His blessing, the matter of being one is further expanded. The urgent necessity for Christian people to be one in Christ, if the world is ever to believe in Him through their testimony and because of the influence of their lives, caused Jesus to pray with desperate earnestness:

"The glory which thou gavest me I have given them; that they may be one, even as we are one: I in them, and thou in me, that they may be made perfect in one; and that the world may know that thou hast sent me, and hast loved them, as thou hast loved me."

The glory of Christ while on earth was to be one with the Father. The glory of the disciples while He was with them was to be one with Christ. The glory of Christians in every succeeding age was to be one with each other, in Christ. As believers grow in Christian unity, the love of God grows in their hearts and the abiding Presence of Christ becomes the most real fact of their lives.

## One Problem, One Remedy

It has been truly said that there is but one problem in life — sin, and one solution of that problem — the gospel of Christ. Sin, however it may be defined and wherever it may be found, causes separation from God. "The angels who neglected their responsibilities and left their own habitation were forever separated from God, and are reserved in everlasting chains under darkness unto the judgment of the great day." The children of Israel, because of their sin of rebellion and stubbornness, were rejected of the Lord and lost their high mission as God's chosen people to bring salvation to the world. The people who lived in the time of Christ and refused to accept Him as the Messiah in the face of the many infallible proofs that were given them, loving darkness rather than light because their deeds were evil, were consigned to eternal darkness, not by the wrath of God but by their own evil choice. During the long years since Jesus was on earth, men and women who refused to repent and accept the gospel of Christ have stumbled in darkness and in due time their feet have slid into everlasting night.

As sin caused separation from God, so the gospel of Christ brings the good news that men may be restored to God's favor, moving from darkness into the light, by the means He has provided. All the barriers to communion with God that sin had raised have been removed in Christ. Through Him and His work of redemption, His life, His teachings, and, most of all, His atoning death, sinners may approach the Light boldly, confidently, unafraid. "For we have not an high priest which cannot be touched with the feeling of our infirmities; but was in all points tempted like as we are, yet without sin. Let us, therefore, come boldly unto the throne of grace, that we may obtain mercy, and find grace to help in time of need."

In view of the universal sinfulness of men and their need for being restored to God's favor, or oneness with God, it is highly significant that Jesus, in His prayer as our High Priest, beseeches His Father that believers may be one with each other as well as one with God. It is as if He were saying in His prayer that He knew that Christian people who could not, or would not, be one with their fellow Christians, could never be one with God. "Let them all be one. Just as you, Father, are in union with me and I with you, let them be in union with us, so that the world may believe that you sent me." (Twenty-first verse, Goodspeed's translation.)

Lack of unity in the Christian life among followers of Christ, therefore, according to these words of Jesus, does two things: first, it prevents complete unity of the believer with God and, second, it nullifies the effect of their witnessing to the world for Christ.

To speak of Christians being united is not necessarily to speak of one church in which all believers shall worship and serve God in the same way. That is, it does not mean that the wiping out of all denominational lines will fulfill the provisions of Christ's prayer. As believers grow in Christian unity, denominational lines will, of themselves, disappear, for they will be no longer important in Christian worship. But to abolish all denominations and bring men and women, who are not united in heart and spirit, into one organization would be a travesty and a farce. The union first must be in things of the spirit and then in outward organizational activities. But the very lack of unity among Christians, often termed "scandalous," has worked overtime in preventing unity with God. However much this judgment may be resented, the pitiful inadequacy of Christian forces in the face of world perils proves it to be true.

What shall be said concerning the nullifying of the Christian witness to the world by the lack of unity among Christian forces? "Why did not Christianity prevent the war with Japan?" a young interned Japanese Christian, who was born in America, asked me. And my reply was that Christianity had not yet prevented American Christians from often being at enmity with one another, because they had never learned that men could not be one with God without being one with their fellow Christians. "If a man say, I love God, and hateth his brother, he is a liar: for he that loveth not his brother whom he hath seen, how can he love God whom he hath not seen?" Lack of unity, evidenced by lack of love, causes the best and most earnest efforts in witnessing for Christ to become as sounding brass and tinkling cymbals. Without spiritual unity of Christians on earth there can be no unity with God in heaven, and hence no complete salvation. And who will heed the testimony of one who does not possess what he is asking others to accept? "When men see Christians really united one with another, as God and Christ are one, and loving one another with the love that reigns in God, they will be convinced of the mission and character of the Saviour." *

## Christian Unity Is Peace

"Mankind can't remain half slave and half free." Nor can man remain half sinner and half saint. It is just as true that followers of Christ cannot continue divided in their Christian lives and attain oneness with God. All that divides men from their fellows in jealousy, suspicion and hatred is sinful. All that unites them in Christ is God's will and His plan for their salvation. In this sense there is no strife that is not

\* *John's Gospel, The Greatest Book in the World*, by Robert E. Speer.

dishonorable and there is no peace that is not honorable. James asks these questions (4:1), "From whence come wars and fightings among you? Come they not hence, even of your lusts that war in your members?" The divisions that have continued to exist among Christian people in all ages bear testimony to the fact that men have never learned the things that belong unto their peace.

The wise man in Proverbs 16:7 says: "When a man's ways please the Lord, he maketh even his enemies to be at peace with him." Here, a way to peace is pointed out that is demonstrably true. A soft answer turneth away wrath. A soft tongue breaketh the bone. A spirit of humility and love disarms our enemies and brings to us peace of heart as well as peaceful relations with our fellowman. In his *Manifest Victory*, J. R. Moseley describes his experience in helping to prevent a lynching during the First World War period. In this hazardous undertaking, he reported that he learned the important lesson that he need fear no one so long as he had a good enough spirit toward him. This reminds us of Isaiah's words to Israel in their dire distress: "Behold, the Lord's hand is not shortened, that it cannot save; neither his ear heavy, that it cannot hear: but your iniquities have separated between you and your God, and your sins have hid his face from you, that he will not hear."

If it be objected that a humble and loving spirit never had any effect on Nazi ruthlessness, the truth of this must be acknowledged. At the same time, it is true that such a pagan and savage philosophy of life could never have laid hold of a great people if they had been treated with sympathy, patience and good will by the so-called Christian nations of the world.

In his *Thinking Aloud in War Time*, Weatherhead tells of a minister who was disturbed in the preparation of a sermon by his little son, who persisted in coming into his study and asking questions. Not wishing to exclude the boy by harsh command, he tore from a magazine a picture of Europe. This he cut into small pieces and gave them to the boy, telling him not to return until he had put the country together. In a surprisingly short time, the youngster reappeared with the job done perfectly. When the father asked how he was able to reassemble the parts so quickly the boy replied: "You see, on the opposite side of the page was the picture of a man. When I got the man right, the country came out right!"

What a parable of life that is! We have been seeking the cause of war in the relationships of countries. The trouble is not with countries, it is with men. When men get right, then countries get right.

When Jesus was born, the angels sang of peace on earth, good will to men. When Jesus bade His followers farewell, He said to them: "Peace I leave with you. My peace I give unto you." And when He prayed for them and for us, He prayed that we might all be one in Him, even as He and the Father are one. Unity in Christ is peace, and the prayer of our Saviour in this seventeenth chapter of John is, therefore, Jesus' prayer for peace.

Sin separates men from God, and when men are

separated from God they are at enmity with one another. Belief in Jesus and acceptance of the gospel opens the way to oneness with God and oneness in spirit with our fellow Christians. We can never expect nations to live at peace with each other until men learn to live at peace with each other. And men will never learn to live at peace with each other until Christians have learned to do so and demonstrate to the world how good and how pleasant it is for brethren to dwell together in unity. If Christ's prayer for peace is answered, it must first be answered in your heart and in mine, then in our personal relationships with our fellow men, and only then in the relationship of our group or nation to other groups or nations. Either Christianity is what it claims to be, or it is a false religion. If it is false, it should be rejected entirely. If it is true, it should be given first place in all that we are and do. Jesus would not have prayed so desperately for unity among Christians were it not necessary for Christian people to be one in heart and spirit if His kingdom is to come and His will be done on earth as it is in heaven.

The supreme question, therefore, that confronts every Christian is: What can I do to make the prayer of Jesus an answered prayer in my life and experience? Every enmity with my fellow man that I slay removes a barrier to communion and peace with God. Every reconciliation I make with an estranged fellow man becomes a vastly important act on behalf of peace in the world. The ideal of a world at peace is no more unattainable than the ideal of a world saved. "For God sent not his Son into the world to condemn the world but that the world through him might be saved." This ideal may seem to be far, far distant in the future, but the Light is still shining in the darkness, for the darkness has never put it out.

## XVIII

## DARKNESS AT ITS WORST

THERE IS comfort in knowing the truth about a situation, however terrible the truth may seem. Uncertainty, dread of what might come, fear of the unknown, these have caused more panic, more of what the Bible calls "fainting," than any accurate knowledge which enables one to face a situation, however bad, and prepare for it.

In the eighteenth chapter of John we see darkness at its worst. We see the Hosts of Darkness mobilized for an all-out assault upon the Light and all who dwelt in the Light. We see their strength, their methods, their cruelty and their failure. Therefore our knowledge of what Darkness was and did at its worst is a continual warning of what Darkness is capable of doing to us individually. At the same time, the failure of Darkness in its supreme effort should give Christians courage to face any foe and to meet any situation when the Captain of our salvation is at our side and when we abide in Him.

Jesus and His disciples had left the city on this last night of His earthly life, crossed the brook Cedron and ascended the slopes of Olivet to the Garden of Gethsemane. Cedron appears as Kidron elsewhere than in the Authorized Version and suggests, in Greek, cedar trees. A brook with cedar trees overshadowing it is a pleasant picture but one which does not fit this scene. The "brook" was in fact a ravine, perhaps dry in the summer and a rushing torrent in the winter. The word Kidron, indeed, signifies a dark stream but not one darkened by cedars. David Smith suggests that the dark color was caused by draining into it the blood of sacrificial victims, and that in April, when the little company crossed into the garden, the ravine was still flooded with the winter rains, the water being darkened by the blood of the paschal lambs which had been recently slain by the thousands at the altar in the Temple court. Thus the "brook" fitted dramatically into the darkness of the night.

John does not tell of the prayer of Jesus, nor the weary watching and sleep of the apostles. Instead, he immediately brings into the picture the first assault of those forces the Prince of Darkness chose to use.

## The Instruments of Satan

The attack was directed against Jesus — Darkness against Light — but men were used as tools of Darkness, and the attack on the Light brought portentous results to all who were associated with Jesus, both those on His side and those against Him.

Judas is mentioned first: "Judas also, which betrayed him, knew the place: for Jesus oftentimes resorted thither with his disciples. Judas then, having received a band of men and officers from the chief priests and Pharisees, cometh thither with lanterns and torches and weapons." These were not merely officers of the Jewish Court, the Sanhedrin, but were Roman soldiers from the garrison, a portion of the detachment which had been sent to Jerusalem to keep peace and order among the Jews during their great Feast of the Passover. Judas came with this company of soldiers and Jewish people, pointed out Jesus to them, and stood with them while Jesus was being arrested.

Judas was "the son of perdition" not because he was a mere pawn in a cosmic event but from his own choice. He loved darkness rather than light because his deeds were evil. He was a thief and stole from the pitiably small common treasury of the apostolic band. He had been denounced as a devil by the Lord even as early as the time of Peter's confession in the synagogue at Capernaum following the miracle of feeding the five thousand. No man becomes a son of perdition by one false step, or one misguided choice. It is the accumulation of small and apparently unimportant sins, the building up of a character black as the night itself through weeks and months of evil thoughts, words and acts that causes a man's final damnation, and such sent Judas to his own place. All the attempts of romanticists to make a hero of Judas instead of a traitor to the Son of God have failed to awaken response in the hearts of Children of Light.

The members of the Jewish official family, including Annas, the ex-high priest; Caiaphas, his son-in-law and present high priest, the members of the Sanhedrin, and the court officers yielded themselves to the devil as his instruments with furious and unholy glee. There is no darker incident in human history than the treatment Jesus received from the time of His arrest to the time of His crucifixion. The implacable enmity of darkness against light, its total lack of anything just, sympathetic or humane in its manner and methods, its unfeeling brutality and stark cruelty, these qualities were displayed in all their horror by the Jews, and later by the Romans, in their treatment of the one perfect Man who ever lived upon the earth. He was forced to stand six separate and distinct trials, three ecclesiastical and three civil, though John says nothing about the trial before Herod. The illegalities connected with the trials stand out in such profusion that it does not take a lawyer to discover them. But the details of the illegalities are not important. What is important is that we understand from these trials the nature and methods of sin and come to realize that Darkness, which had no mercy on Jesus, will have no mercy on you and me if we fall into its hands.

The cruelty of the personal treatment Jesus received enables us to see the depths of human depravity. He was insulted, He was spit upon, He was struck in the face while standing trial, He was arrayed in a purple robe and a crown of thorns, He was scourged as only Romans could scourge a helpless victim, He was smitten by soldiers. During the long hours from midnight until the time of the crucifixion at the sixth hour there is no record of His being offered so much as a cup of water or a crust of bread, no mention of one kindly and sympathetic word being spoken to Him. It is no wonder that Pilate, with a mixture of contempt and pity, pointed at Him and said to the shouting crowd: "Behold the man!" which, translated into modern terms, means, "Look at the poor fellow!"

Pilate comes closer to winning a bit of sympathy for himself than any other in the miserable group about Jesus. He was a good enough judge to know that Jesus was innocent, and he saw through the pious pretensions of the priests and scribes. He made a real effort to release Jesus, but he had compromised with sin and evil so long in his life that, when the supreme opportunity of choosing Light came, he could only choose darkness. He delivered Jesus to be crucified, and the judgment of all ages since has been: "He suffered under Pontius Pilate, was crucified, dead and buried."

## The Effect on the Disciples

John is not specific about the effect on the disciples of this all-out assault of Satan, the Prince of Darkness. He mentions Peter and he mentions himself anonymously as "another disciple who was known to the high priest." In the Synoptic Gospels, we read that they all forsook Him and fled. "I have trodden the winepress alone; and of the people there was none with me" (Isaiah 63:3). Those who might have comforted Him in His last hours, and eased the pain of His heart a bit if not the pain and weariness of His body, failed Him when He needed them most. Darkness is too strong for the strongest man who rejects, or neglects, the Light.

Peter and John must have soon recovered a bit of their courage if they were included in the "all" who forsook Him and fled, for we read that they followed Jesus, and John, who was known to the High Priest, went in with Jesus into the palace of the High Priest. Peter stayed at the door without, where the first denial of Christ occurred. Later he joined a group who had gathered round a fire which had been made in a brazier in the court before the palace. Here the second denial took place. Still later, a kinsman of the man whose ear Peter had cut off asked, "Did not I see thee in the garden with him?" Peter then denied again, and immediately the cock crew.

In the gospel according to Mark, which gives Peter's own version of the life of Christ, we read that he began to curse and to swear after the third denial. The other evangelists were willing to forget this, but Peter wanted to forget it never, and he wanted others to know what sin and darkness can make a man do who really loves the Master, if he relaxes his guard.

One of the beautiful Negro spirituals begins each verse with the words, "Were you there when they crucified my Lord?" When we think of Peter, his denials, his cursing and swearing it would be well to make this question more personal: "Was I there when they crucified my Lord? Did I deny Him as Peter did?" How easy it is to slip into a denial today, a denial of the Lord which often requires no words. If I had been in the court before the palace of the high priest, would I have been any braver and stronger than Peter?

The impetuous apostle was physically brave and

would gladly have continued his fight in the Garden until he had been hacked to pieces. But he could not stand ridicule, and the questions that provoked his denials were tinged with both ridicule and contempt. Poor Peter, in this he was not so much worse than many nominal Christians in our own time who "fold up" before adverse public opinion and are willing to deny their Lord to keep from being laughed at, or to retain the favor of those whose good will seems to be of value. The many denials we can find in our own hearts, if not in our words, should keep us from pointing a finger of scorn at this man whose heart was broken when Jesus looked at him after the cock had crowed the second time.

## Light Meeting Darkness

The unruffled calm, the constancy of purpose, the majesty of bearing which characterized the Master in His every contact in this chapter and the one following proved Him to be the Lord of life and death. When the motley mob confronted Him in the garden and He disclosed His identity to them, they involuntarily shrank backward and fell to the ground. There was no physical force that caused them to do this but rather the overpowering moral force of Light in meeting darkness.

When Jesus said, "If therefore ye seek me, let these go their way," He had in mind two purposes. The first was to free the apostles from the physical dangers and spiritual peril which He had to meet; the second was to let it be known that He alone could and must pay the price of redemption from sin. In this sense it was true that Jesus must bear the cross alone and all the world go free. It was for this express purpose that He came into the world.

When Jesus stood before Annas, then before Caiaphas and then before Pilate, it was He who was the real Judge and these highly exalted earthly rulers became the unwitting and unwilling prisoners at the bar. Contrast the attitude and demeanor of our Lord with that of His judges and the truth of this will stand forth in startling clearness. Jesus was calm, composed and courteous. His judges were excited, irritable and implacable. Jesus was without fear, bitterness or hatred. Each of His judges exhibited these unjudicial qualities to such an extent as to unfit them for their high office and to cause them to earn the contempt and condemnation of succeeding generations. The whole bearing of Jesus showed Him to be a man of bravery, purity, and consecration—yea more than a man, even God incarnated in human flesh. The bearing of His judges showed that Satan had clothed himself with them, even as it is said in Judges that the Holy Spirit clothed Himself with Gideon.

Pilate made more than one attempt to call forth mercy and pity in the hearts of the shouting people. He gave them the choice between Jesus and Barabbas. Since it was his custom to release a prisoner in honor of the Feast, he hoped they would choose Jesus. But they chose Barabbas, who was a robber and notorious among those who were yelling for the blood of Jesus. Pilate thrust the exhausted human body of Jesus in front of the frenzied crowd, a crown of thorns on His bleeding head and a scarlet robe over His quivering body, and said, "Look at the poor fellow!" Incited by the chief priest and officers, the people cried out, "Crucify him, crucify him!"

Long, long years before, the law of Moses had warned the people not to follow a multitude to do evil. An implicit understanding of the dangers of mob psychology is contained in this command, but this frenzied crowd of people seemed bent only on being the instrument of Satan, and the well-known warning was forgotten. From our vantage point of succeeding centuries, we can look back to the "poor fellow" standing in front of the howling mob and see the scene transformed so that through faith it becomes to us what it had always been to God.

> "The head that once was crowned with thorns
> Is crowned with glory now;
> A royal diadem adorns
> The holy victor's brow!"

The dawn of the day of the crucifixion brought no light into this scene of darkness. The sun shone on in the heavens until, according to Matthew, at the sixth hour it gave up its daily attempt to bring light and gladness to mankind and there was darkness over the land until the ninth hour. Darkness held full sway for three hours and seemed to be the victor. The agonizing cry of Jesus, "My God, my God, why hast thou forsaken me?," wrung from a crucified spirit as well as a broken body, brings to our consciousness the awful significance of the hour as nothing else could. God had made Him to become sin for us, who knew no sin. The cup which His Father gave Him, He drank to the dregs. Darkness at its worst killed His body and caused agony to His soul. It had then done all that it could and found itself defeated. The words of Jesus, "It is finished," pronounced the doom of Satan, put to flight the Hosts of Darkness, and opened up to mankind a sure and safe pathway to eternal Light.

> "Finished all the types and shadows
>   Of the ceremonial law;
> Finished, all that God had promised,
> Death and hell no more shall awe.
>   It is finished!
> Saints, from hence your comforts draw."

## XIX

## CRUCIFIED, DEAD AND BURIED

When Darkness had done its worst, the Lord of Glory had been crucified and, being dead, was put into a tomb, the door of which was closed with a great stone and sealed with the authority of the Roman government. Was there one who believed that Jesus would ever rise again?

The Sabbath day during which His lifeless body lay in the sepulchre must have been a day of deepest gloom to the little company of men and women who loved Him, and who believed in Him. "We trusted that it had been he which should have delivered Israel." Perhaps during those long hours of despair they thought of the words He had spoken to them about His death and tried to understand what He had meant when He said that as Moses lifted up the serpent in the wilderness even so must the Son of man be lifted up. Maybe they were in no mental or spiritual condition to understand, and certainly they were utterly unable to work out a satisfying theology for themselves which included in it the death of the Son of God. But as we look back across the centuries to the little skull-shaped mound outside the city walls and see hanging there the lifeless body of Him whom our soul loveth, we must understand, in some measure at least, why He thus died, or we are in danger of missing the salvation He has provided.

## The Crucifixion As Seen by John

When we remember that John's was the last account of the gospel to be written, and that John was a very old man when he set down the facts of the crucifixion remaining uppermost in his mind after the passing of the years, we will appreciate more the precious value of the few details he has given. John had stood closest to the cross at the last, so close that Jesus spoke to him and gave His mother into the keeping of the beloved apostle.

When Pilate finally yielded to the implacable fury and hate of the leaders of the people, he passed sentence of death upon Jesus and handed Him over to them to be crucified. It was the Roman custom to compel the victim to carry his cross to the place of execution, outside the city's walls. The name of the victim and his crime were inscribed on a board and nailed to the cross above his head. In the case of the two thieves who were crucified with Jesus — one on the right and one on the left — the word "robber" would appear after their names. But Pilate saw a way of showing his contempt for the Jews and getting at least some revenge on his tormentors, so he wrote on the board after the name of Jesus, not rebel or traitor, but "King of the Jews." There is grim irony in this, for it was in very fact the charge they made against Him, crying out: "We have no king but Cæsar." The chief priests were indignant, and more especially because the inscription was in three languages, Hebrew, Greek, and Latin, so that all might be able to read it. Their protest to Pilate was met with disdain and an assertion of authority that might better have been used before he turned the innocent victim over to the pack of angry wolves: "What I have written, I have written!"

The four soldiers who carried out the execution of Jesus divided His garments among themselves. Finding that His coat, or "The Robe," was woven without seam, they cast lots for it, thus fulfilling the ancient prophecy found in Psalm 22:18: "They parted my raiment among them, and for my vesture they did cast lots."

Seven sayings, or words, from the cross are recorded in the four gospels. Of these, John gives three. The first is the very precious consignment of Mary, His mother, to John the beloved:

"When Jesus therefore saw his mother, and the disciple standing by, whom he loved, he saith unto his mother, Woman, behold thy son! Then saith he to the disciple, Behold thy mother! And from that hour that disciple took her unto his own home."

The second is the words, "I thirst," usually spoken of as the cry of suffering humanity. However, these words were immediately spoken in order that He might receive the vinegar, or sour wine, provided for the purpose of clearing His throat parched with suffering. This was not the stupefying drink that had been refused earlier. When He received the drink, He cried out with a loud voice, "It is finished!" The other evangelists tell us of the loud cry. Only John records what was said. It is thus plain that John believed Jesus took the drink in order that His voice might be heard and His last words understood by the crowd which stood around the cross and those who looked on from a distance.

The Jewish authorities, having omitted the weightier matters of the law, justice, mercy and faith, were still very zealous about the minor matters. Their Sabbath day must not be defiled by permitting the dead bodies to remain on the crosses and unburied for even a moment after sundown on Friday. They requested of Pilate that the soldiers break the legs of the victims in order to hasten their death. This was done in the case of the two thieves, but when the soldiers came to Jesus, He was already dead. They did not break His legs but instead pierced His side with a spear and forthwith there came out blood and water.

It is evident that John attached great importance to this incident, for he emphasized the fact that he himself saw it, and that he knew what he said was true. To John it was a proof of the physical death of Jesus. This was no mere swooning, or a pretended death. John desired men in all ages to keep in mind his personal testimony that Jesus was indeed dead. But he seemed to find something else in the flow of blood and water from the pierced side of the Saviour. After the passing of the years, the blood had become to him the "Blood of the New Covenant," and the water stood for the washing of regeneration, the cleansing element of baptism.

The simple funeral services of the Master are pictured in the five concluding verses of the chapter. Joseph of Arimathea, a secret disciple, and Nicodemus took the body of Jesus and prepared it for burial according to Jewish custom, using a mixture of myrrh and aloes, about an hundred-pound weight, and wrapping the body in a sheet. It is well to remember these facts of the preparation of the body for burial when we look into the tomb later for evidences of the Resurrection. Near the place where Jesus was crucified there was a garden, and in the garden a new sepulchre wherein was never man yet laid. The rule was that the mangled bodies of crucified criminals should be cast into the loathsome pit of Gehenna, and this would have been done with the body of Jesus if the two men, Joseph possessed of wealth, and Nicodemus possessed of influence, had not intervened with Pilate and received permission to bury the body.

The Light that shineth in the darkness was very dim,

now. Could it be that the Darkness was about to put it out?

## The Necessity Laid upon Jesus

Now that we have considered the facts of the crucifixion, death, and burial of Jesus, it is time to ask, and attempt to answer, the question: Why did Jesus have to go through all this humiliation and suffering? What was the necessity laid upon Him? It was one that He voluntarily assumed and not one that was forced upon Him. But it was no less a necessity and without it there would have been no salvation for mankind. His words to Nicodemus in the third chapter answer this question: "As Moses lifted up the serpent in the wilderness, even so must the Son of man be lifted up." And in the twelfth chapter, He said: "And I, if I be lifted up from the earth, will draw all men unto me."

The crucifixion of Jesus, in God's redemptive plans, accomplished in general four things — in particular many other things that cannot here be enumerated:

### (a) Drew the Attention of All Men

The reference to the Old Testament incident of the plague of fiery serpents and the remedy for their poisonous bite recalled to the minds of the people a vivid experience the children of Israel had during their wanderings in the wilderness. The serpents had been sent as a punishment for the rebellion and disobedience of the people. The remedy was a brazen serpent, set on a pole which was lifted up in the midst of the camp, to which the stricken people were directed to lift up their eyes. "And it came to pass, that if a serpent had bitten any man, when he beheld the serpent of brass, he lived" (Numbers 21:9).

Being lifted up, in the case of Jesus, meant death, a shameful, cruel death on a cross. More even than His perfect life, His death for crimes He had not done has made Him conspicuous among all the peoples of the world. If He had lived as He did live, and had taught as He did teach, without His death on the Cross, it is doubtful that He would have commanded very much more attention or secured a more permanent place in the memory and affection of mankind than other great teachers of the world. But there is no other fact in history so securely fastened in the minds, if not in the hearts, of men as the Cross, and Christ lifted upon it.

One of the organists in the Grand Central Station, New York City, who plays the songs requested by the thousands of men and women in the armed forces who pass through that great clearing house, has recently stated in a radio talk that the song most often requested — more than any tune on the "Hit Parade" or any popular war song — is "The Old Rugged Cross." Whether men accept Christ or not, He has drawn their attention and they recognize that His claims must be dealt with. It is heartening to know that those who fight our battles love the "Old Rugged Cross."

### (b) *To Expose the Nature of Sin*

In no other way could the nature of sin be revealed so unmistakably to men than by the crucifixion of the one perfect Man who ever lived upon the earth. We have seen already that there is no mercy, no sympathy, no justice, no decency in sin, and none of these qualities are found in the treatment Jesus received. The fact that He possessed all His adorable attributes in a superlative and unalterable way had no effect on sin, its nature or its methods. Darkness set upon the Light with all fury to put It out forever. Wherever there is light, darkness is against it and all compromises darkness may seem to make are for the purpose of more effectively, at the last, extinguishing every vestige of light. Sinful men always love darkness rather than light, because their deeds are evil. If darkness had succeeded in putting out The Light, then the world would have been forever enveloped in thick gloom. It failed in this supreme attempt, thank God, but, ever since, sin has been at its appointed work of extinguishing light wherever it can and luring men into its shadows so that they might stumble to destruction. The wages of sin is death, and these wages have never been reduced nor changed.

If men could once be made to realize that the analogy of a biting fiery serpent correctly represents the nature and methods of every sin, they would not think of sin lightly, nor speak of little sins as if these were of no consequence.

### (c) *To Provide a Way of Escape for Sinners*

It was not a bitten Israelite that God commanded Moses to lift up on a pole for the people to see, nor the image of one. Instead, it was a brazen serpent representing the very plague itself that was causing them suffering and death. Now Paul tells us that Christ was made to become sin for us, He who knew no sin. In some mysterious and awful way, the Son of God was lifted up and slain, not as a sinner but as sin itself. This fact goes too deep for human understanding, but in it we can see some of the reasons for His spiritual agony and understand in a small measure the meaning of the cry: "My God, my God, why hast thou forsaken me?" Can it be that for one instant of time the Light went out entirely, in order that It might shine more brightly for men throughout all future ages?

The Apostle Peter tells us that Jesus, His own self, bare our sins in His own body on the tree, that we, being dead to sin, might live unto righteousness: by whose stripes we are healed. And again he says: "Forasmuch as ye know that ye were not redeemed with corruptible things, as silver and gold, from your vain conversation received by tradition from your fathers; but with the precious blood of Christ, as of a lamb without blemish and without spot." These verses give us the fact, the theory and the glorious results of our Lord's atoning sacrifice.

> "There was none other good enough
> To pay the price of sin.
> He only could unlock the door
> Of Heaven and let us in."

### (d) *To Provide a Garment of Righteousness for Those Who Will Accept It*

If our Master's atoning death provided only an escape from sin and nothing more, it would have been incomplete. But men who believe in Christ and accept His way of salvation receive both pardon of their sins and a clear and indisputable title to eternal life. He has provided a garment of righteousness which pardoned sinners receive as a free gift, through faith. When God looks upon a pardoned sinner, He sees not the sinner but the righteousness of His Son in which the sinner is clothed. This righteousness is one that the sinner could not provide for himself, no matter how earnest and consecrated he might be in his Christian life.

> "When He shall come with trumpet sound,
> Oh, may I then in Him be found,
> Clothed in His righteousness alone,
> Faultless to stand before the Throne."

The closer we come to Christ as we grow and develop in the Christian life, the more we see that all our righteousness is as "filthy rags," and the more joyously we accept the beauteous garment that He has prepared for us.

The way of salvation is open to every repentant sinner. The conditions imposed are so simple they are sometimes lightly regarded. They are so profound they satisfy all the requirements of a holy God who cannot look upon sin with any degree of allowance, nor lightly cleanse the guilty.

"Are you washed in the blood of the Lamb?"

## XX

## GOOD MORNING!

In his fine commentary on John, Marcus Dods points out that the beloved apostle gives us no narrative of the Resurrection itself, but, rather, that which is more valuable, a brief account of the way in which he, himself, was convinced that a resurrection had taken place. John could have given personal testimony of many other evidences, but those he sets forth are simple, convincing and sufficient. His method here, as in all the gospel account he wrote, is selective. "Many other things truly did Jesus in the presence of his disciples, which are not written in this book: but these are written, that ye might believe that Jesus is the Christ, the Son of God; and that believing ye might have life through his name."

In the first chapter of this book, it was noted that the translation of John 1:5 by Dr. Goodspeed was its inspiration and theme: "The Light is still shining in the darkness, for the darkness has never put it out." This same New Testament scholar renders the salutation of Jesus to Mary in Matthew 28:9, which appears in the King James Version as "All hail!": "Good morning!" Three hundred and more years ago, when the older translation was made, the words, "All hail," were, doubtless, a familiar form of greeting. Today, they sound to us unfamiliar, far away and stilted. But the words, "Good morning!" bring the greeting of the

Risen Lord right into our everyday lives. There is perhaps no other greeting so commonly used by men as this.

After the darkness of the crucifixion and the two nights and a day that followed it, the words, "Good Morning," spoken by Him who was dead and was alive again, brought joy unspeakable and full of glory to Mary. Though twenty centuries have passed since they were spoken, they continue to bring joy to the hearts of people that walk in darkness, for, hearing them, through faith those in darkness see a great light.

## The Evidence

It is interesting to note, and not without significance, that Mary Magdalene bulks larger in the chapter John devotes to the Resurrection than any other witness. Throughout the first eighteen verses, out of a total of thirty-one verses, this woman of Magdala plays the leading part. She had been a great sinner, for both Matthew and Mark tell us that she was one out of whom the Lord cast seven devils. However, there is no evidence whatever that she was once a habitual sinner against the seventh commandment. Because the Lord had done so much for her, she seemed to have loved Him more deeply and more understandingly than any of the others. "She was last at His Cross, and first at His grave. She stayed longest *there* and was sooner *here*. She sought Him while it was yet dark, even before she had light to seek Him by." (Bishop Andrews, quoted in Ryle's *Expository Thoughts on the Gospels*.)

When Mary Magdalene found that the stone had

been rolled away from the sepulchre, she ran to tell Peter and John. It may have been that a group of women, Mary Magdalene, the other Mary, Salome, and others, together with the Apostles Peter and John, had been staying near the place of burial outside the city, perhaps with friends, so that they might reach the tomb early before the opening of the city gates and the stirring of the people on Sunday morning. Peter and John ran to the tomb, their running seeming to indicate that they were not very far away when they received the news. John, being the younger of the two, outran Peter, came to the sepulchre first, stooped down and saw the linen cloths lying. But he did not go in. When Peter arrived, he went into the tomb and examined the evidence he found. This evidence convinced the two men that Jesus had risen, and after the passing of a half century or more the details remained, as it were, photographed in John's mind.

The absence of the body of Jesus was not the sole evidence that brought belief to John and Peter. They saw the linen clothes lying and the napkin, that was about His head, not lying with the linen clothes, but wrapped together (or folded) in a place by itself. John had previously stated that the body of Jesus was prepared for burial with a hundred pounds of myrrh and aloes, wound in linen clothes with the spices. Myrrh, which was a thick fluid, according to Chrysostom who lived in the fourth century, glues the cloth to the body not less firmly than lead. If the body had been stolen from the tomb, those who stole it would not have taken the time and trouble to remove the cloth before bearing the body away. Indeed, after a lapse of time the cloth could not be removed at all without mutilating the body.

But the evidence of the burial clothes shows more than the fact that the body was not stolen. The napkin from the head lay apart from the linen that had been wound around the body. There was no disorder, there were no rents in the cloth, there was no disarray. Jesus had risen from the dead, and the burial clothes, no longer containing a body, had fallen back to the floor of the tomb. The napkin, which had been on His head, was thus *apart* from the linen clothes. This is the evidence that John says convinced him. When rightly understood, it is as convincing evidence as the mind of man could desire.

The two apostles left the tomb and returned to Jerusalem unto their own home. The place they had been staying in Jerusalem during those troubled days was the "home" referred to by John. It may have been the same house where the Last Supper was celebrated, and at this house Mary the mother of Jesus would be, for John tells us that, after the words of Jesus on the Cross, he took Mary into his own home from that hour. The two would want to bring the news to Mary first.

Mary Magdalene remained at the sepulchre, weeping. Her tears were not tears of joy that her Master had risen from the dead. They were tears of sorrow that the old relationships of life were gone, never to return. She had not been convinced by the evidence of the grave clothes. When the two angels, whom she saw sitting, one at the head, and the other at the foot, where the body of Jesus had lain, asked why she wept, she replied: "Because they have taken away my Lord, and I know not where they have lain him." Even when Jesus Himself spoke to her, saying, "Woman, why weepest thou? Whom seekest thou?" not recognizing Him, she pleaded with piteous sobs: "Sir, if thou have borne him hence, tell me where thou hast laid him, and I will take him away."

This pathetic scene was transformed utterly by the Risen Lord speaking one word — "Mary." She doubtless had not looked at Him closely before, her eyes being dimmed with tears, for she then turned herself at the sound of her name pronounced by a familiar voice and cried: "My Master!" However, it is quite evident that Mary did not, as yet, have full faith that He was risen. Instead, by her word of greeting, which was a common one in Galilee, and by her actions, indicated by Jesus' warning that old relationships could not be resumed, she seemed to believe that it had all been a terrible dream, Jesus was not dead at all, and everything would be the same as it had been. It was to startle her out of this kind of thinking and feeling that Jesus spoke to her the words, "Touch me not" (the Greek tense suggests the translation, "Stop touching me," or "Stop holding on to me"); for I am not yet ascended to my Father: but go to my brethren and say unto them, I ascend unto my Father, and your Father; and to my God, and your God." These words have troubled many readers of John, but their meaning and intent ought to be very plain indeed. Mary then obeyed the words of Jesus, and reported the whole matter to the disciples.

The evening of that same day, the disciples were together — probably in the same Upper Room — and the doors were shut for fear of the Jews. They must have been discussing in an eager and excited way the things that had been reported to them, and Peter and John probably told many times the things they had seen.

Then Jesus came and stood in their midst, saying, "Peace be unto you," and showing them the wound prints in His hands and side. The disciples recognized Him now and were glad when they saw the Lord. How did He enter a room whose doors and windows were shut? Perhaps it is nearer the truth to say He did not enter at all. He was there all the time. Long before, He had said, "Where two or three are gathered together in my name, there am I in the midst of them." Now, being present, He merely made Himself manifest to the disciples in His resurrection body.

There are two ways by which the eye of man may be enabled to see spiritual realities: the vision of man may be "stepped up" so that it includes spiritual things, or the spiritual realities may be "stepped down" into the range of mortal vision. Here in the Upper Room, the spiritual body of Jesus came within the range of mortal vision, and the disciples were glad when they saw the Lord. They must have met together many times before the next manifestation eight days later. Each time they were on a tiptoe of expectancy: "Maybe He will be here tonight." The fact that Jesus appeared, disappeared, and appeared again during the forty days He was on earth before the ascension taught the disciples the lesson that He was always in the midst of those who gathered in His name. Sometimes He manifested Himself, and sometimes their spiritual state was such that they felt His Presence without seeing His form. So it is with disciples in our day. Francis Thompson, in "In No Strange Land," has expressed beautifully this truth:

> "The angels keep their ancient places; —
> Turn but a stone and start a wing!
> 'Tis ye, 'tis your estranged faces,
> That miss the many-splendored thing.
>
> "But (when so sad thou canst not sadder)
> Cry; and upon Thy so sore loss
> Shall shine the traffic of Jacob's ladder
> Pitched between Heaven and Charing Cross.
>
> "Yea, in the night my soul, my daughter,
> Cry, clinging heaven by the hems,
> And lo, Christ walking on the water,
> Not of Gennesaret, but Thames!"

When Jesus appeared first to the little group in the Upper Room, Thomas was not present. All the testimony of those who had seen Him would not convince the doubter. "I will not believe," said he, "except I shall see in his hands the print of the nails, and thrust my hand into his side."

The next Sunday — or eight days later according to the Jewish method of counting — Jesus appeared again to the group and this time Thomas was with them.

The greeting, "Peace be unto you," being said, Jesus spoke to Thomas: "Reach hither thy finger, and behold my hands; and reach hither thy hand, and thrust it into my side: and be not faithless but believing." These words were enough for Thomas, and he cried out, "My Lord and my God." The last doubter among the disciples had come to faith. Then Jesus pronounced a blessing upon those who have not seen and yet have believed, a blessing which included all the faithful Christians who have lived since His ascension.

John concludes his gospel with this account of the facts that had convinced him Christ was risen from the dead. The twenty-first chapter is a postscript, or epilogue — a later addition to the Gospel that was made for certain specific purposes.

## All Clear

The world has grown sadly familiar with black-outs during a war in which fighting so largely took place in the air. The "black-out" of the crucifixion is better understood, and its awful significance more completely realized, after the horrors of the most terrible war the world has known have been experienced all over the earth. The words "All Clear" have now significance, not only in war, but in the whole of life. They stand both for the passing of danger and for safety in resuming life and activity in the open and in light where men have a God-given right to be.

When Jesus spoke to Mary on the morning of the Resurrection and said, "Good morning," He was giving her and the disciples through her the "All Clear" signal in their Christian life and work. He was doing the same thing when He appeared to the disciples in the Upper Room and greeted them, "Peace be unto you."

It is said that the news of Wellington's victory at Waterloo was brought to England by sailing ship to the south coast, and from there wigwagged by semaphore to London. The semaphore on the roof of Winchester Cathedral picked up the message and began to spell it out, "Wellington Defeated," and the fog closed in so that the semaphore could not be seen. The incompleted message, with its sad news of the defeat of the great English general, was carried to London, where it caused the deepest gloom. Then the fog broke and the cathedral was seen to be still working, "Wellington defeated the enemy." The joy that spread over England was all the greater because of the preceding gloom. This story illustrates the effect of Calvary and the Resurrection on the apostles, and on the world. The fog of despair and gloom settled down on men when Jesus died. The fog lifted on Easter morning, and the ancient semaphore spelled out its completed message: "Jesus defeated sin and death." The "All Clear" signal had sounded. Death and hell no more shall terrify and awe those who believe in the Lord of Life and Death.

The Light is still shining in the darkness for the darkness has never put it out.

# XXI

# AN IMPERISHABLE POSTSCRIPT

It is evident from the closing verses of the twentieth chapter that the apostle originally closed his account of the Gospel at this point. Later, the twenty-first chapter was added as a kind of postscript, or epilogue. If this postscript had not been added, the account would have been complete, but Christianity would have been immeasurably poorer, for it contains some very precious incidents, nowhere else related, which occurred in the forty-day period between the Resurrection and the Ascension.

The chapter seems to have been written with three distinct purposes in mind, and is indeed closer in spirit and purpose to the first chapter of Acts than to the twentieth chapter of John. In it we see the precarious position the Church at first occupied, and we are ourselves encouraged when we note that the apostles, with the earthly companionship of Jesus just recently removed, were subject to human temptations and beset with weakness and indecision even as Christian men and women are still.

## Seek Ye First the Kingdom of God

When the Passover season was over, it was but natural that the apostles should return to their homes in Galilee. They would be drawn together frequently to talk over the awe-inspiring events they had witnessed, and one day there were seven of them who met together, perhaps at the house of the old fisherman, Zebedee. John gives the identity of five of these — Peter, Thomas, Nathanael, and the sons of Zebedee, James and John, adding "and two other of his disciples." Very likely they stood on the shores of the lake and watched the fishing boats leaving the land for the familiar fishing places. Their lives were yet without direction and lacking in a compelling inner power. They did not know what had become of Jesus, and it may have been weeks since His last appearance to them. Marcus Dods notes that they already had in their possession all the facts they were later to use for the conversion of the world. But they had no impulse to proclaim the truth. This was to come to them later, at the Day of Pentecost. Just now they were "driven of the waves and tossed, double-minded men, unstable in all their ways." Finally, Peter could stand it no longer and cried out, "I'm going fishing!" That was all the others needed to hear, and they replied, "We are going with you." Though there was no harm in their going fishing, this action seems to have been perilously similar to the futile attitude Thomas expressed when Jesus spoke of going again to Judea on receiving the news of Lazarus' death: "What's the use? Let us go and die with Him." The apostles seemed to be slipping back into the familiar grooves of their old lives, there to remain as unknown and uninspired fishermen. It was from this that Jesus saved them by another appearance in His resurrection body, after a fruitless night of fishing.

These apostles were experienced fishermen, and the fact that they caught nothing during the night must have added to the confusion of their minds and hearts. In the early morning light they saw someone on the shore, who called out to them, "Children, have ye any meat?" or, as we would say, "Boys, have you caught anything?" They answered, "No," without recognizing Jesus, and He spoke to them again, directing them where and how to fish. Following His directions, they gathered so many fish in the net that they were unable to haul it in. John then said to Peter, "It is the Lord," and Peter, putting on his fisher's coat, jumped into the water to hasten their approach to the land. In that one haul 153 fish were caught, yet the net held. When the apostles reached the shore, breakfast was already prepared for them, and Jesus bade them come and eat.

Here, in an unforgettable way, Jesus illustrated the truth of His words: "Seek ye first the kingdom of God and his righteousness, and all these things shall be added unto you." If we had taken the lesson to heart, our lives and our experience as Christians would have been transformed. In seeking to do our own will, or in drifting aimlessly in life, our nets have been empty and our lives barren. James puts his finger on the trouble when he writes, "You crave things and cannot have them and so you commit murder. You covet things and cannot get them and so you quarrel and fight. You do not have things, because you do not ask for them. You ask and fail to get them, because you ask with wrong motives, to spend them on your pleasures" (James 4:2, 3 — Goodspeed).

The apostles never forgot the lesson of this miracle — the only one recorded — after the Resurrection. From that time on, they sought His Kingdom and His righteousness, and the necessary things of life to make them useful servants of the King were added unto them. If we had more faith our own lives would be more fruitful and more satisfying.

### The Restoration of Peter

Peter had already been restored to his close personal relationship with Christ in an interview not mentioned in the Gospel records, but spoken of in I Corinthians, fifteenth chapter. On this never-to-be-forgotten morning, he was restored officially as an apostle.

After breakfast — it is not stated that Jesus partook of the food — the Master turned to Peter and began questioning him. Though the conversation took place in the presence of the other apostles, Jesus showed the utmost consideration in handling the man who found it so difficult to be transformed into a rock. Three times Peter was asked the question by his Master, "Lovest thou me?" and each time, following his reply, was given an instruction which was an advance on the preceding instruction.

It is difficult to put into English the different shades of meaning which the original Greek expresses so clearly. Jesus asked Peter the first time if he loved Him more devotedly than the others did. Peter replied — using an entirely different word for love — "Thou knowest that I love thee," that is, "have an affection for you." The second time Jesus asked the question,

He used the same word for love as before, but omitted the comparison with the others. Peter made exactly the same reply he made to the first question. Jesus then used Peter's word for love and asked, "Simon, son of Jonas, do you have an affection for me?" Peter was grieved, both because the three questions reminded him of his three denials, and also because the Master seemed now not only to question his devotion but also his affection. He replied, "Lord, thou knowest all things, thou knowest that I love thee." The Lord did know it, and His prayer that Peter's faith fail not had been answered.

The instruction given the apostle after the first question and answer was, "Feed my lambs." This was an important charge but not an exceedingly difficult one, for lambs are ready to receive the food offered them. The "little ones," in the Church and Kingdom are the least difficult and most satisfying members with whom to work. The second instruction was: "Tend my sheep," or "Be a shepherd to my sheep." This is a harder task than the first, more heartbreaking and requiring more patience. The third instruction was, "Feed my sheep." This is the hardest task of all, as all workers in adult education will testify. The sheep often do not know what they want, and sometimes are unwilling to be fed at all. The task of feeding them was given to Peter and is the task of every pastor and teacher today. We must learn better methods of feeding the sheep, else the Kingdom will be long delayed, for it is always the adults of the world who are in charge of its affairs and not the "lambs," or children.

After giving the apostle these important instructions, Jesus reveals to him something of what the future held in store for him: "When thou wast young, thou girdst thyself, and walkest whither thou wouldst: but when thou shalt be old, thou shalt stretch forth thy hands, and another shall gird thee, and carry thee whither thou wouldst not." John adds that Jesus said this, signifying by what death Peter should glorify God.

On the Appian Way, leading out of Rome, is "Quo Vadis Chapel." This chapel commemorates the legend that Peter was fleeing from Rome during the persecution by Nero and met Jesus on the Appian Way. He cried out *"Quo Vadis, Domine"* — "Whither goest Thou, Lord," and received the reply, "Back to Rome to be crucified in thy stead." Peter turned back, and when his time came to die, requested that he be crucified head downward, since he was not worthy to die in the same manner as his Lord.

### The Future of John

A third reason for the postscript was to destroy the legend, which was becoming widespread, that John should never die. Then, as now, people were eager to lay hold of something mysterious and magnify it.

When Peter had been told the solemn experiences awaiting him, he saw John near by and asked, "Lord and what shall this man do?" The reply of Jesus was a rebuke to Peter and to all future disciples who seek to condition, modify or guide their actions by what others do. "If I will that he tarry till I come, what is that to thee? Follow thou me?" In other words, Jesus is saying in effect to Peter that what John does is not his concern and that he should not be over-solicitous about it. His task and duty are to follow Jesus, no matter what others may do. This is the kind of discipline that is enforced in the army of victorious nations. Because it has not been enforced, and often seems not even to be understood, the victory of the army of the Lord has been too long delayed.

What the future of John was to be, Jesus did not say. But He gave no grounds for the belief that rapidly grew up that John was to be a "wandering Jew," living through the centuries and tarrying until Jesus came to earth again. This superstition John himself emphatically repudiated. The Church would be stronger and purer if it had repudiated with equal emphasis other superstitions which have sprung up through the succeeding centuries.

John closed this epilogue with his personal testimony that the things he has written were true and were so recognized by those acquainted with the facts of Jesus' life. He then repeated the statement he had made at the conclusion of the twentieth chapter, that there were many other things Jesus did which might have been written but had been omitted for the sake of brevity. His purpose of proving that Jesus is the Christ, the Son of God, and that believing men might have life through His name, had been accomplished. Nothing more needed to be added. The record was complete, convincing and satisfying to all who will to do His will.

"There is a remarkable legend that when the Lord gave the Law from Sinai He wrought great marvels with His voice (Job 18:5). The voice sounded from the South, and as the people hasted to the South, lo! it sounded from the North. They turned to the North and it came from the East. They turned to the East and it came from the West. They turned thither and it came from heaven. They lifted up their eyes to heaven and it came from the depths of the earth. And they said one to the other, 'Where shall wisdom be found?' (Job 28:12). And the voice went out throughout the world and was divided into seventy voices, according to the seventy tongues of men, and each nation heard the Voice in its own tongue and their souls failed them, but Israel heard and suffered not. And each one in Israel heard it according to his capacity, and men and youths and boys and sucklings and women; His voice was to each one as each one had the power to receive it. The student of St. John will find the parable fulfilled as he ponders the Apostle's words with growing experience and unchanged patience. He himself limits the meaning that he finds in them." *

The last instruction Jesus gave was contained in His words to Peter, "Follow me."

> "Finding, following, keeping, struggling,
> Is He sure to bless?
> Saints, apostles, prophets, martyrs
> Answer: 'Yes!' "

The Light is still shining in the darkness, for the darkness has never put it out!

* Quoted in *John's Gospel, The Greatest Book in the World,* by Robert Speer.